Praise for *Is This Seat Taken?*
It's Never Too Late to Find the Right Seat

"This entertaining book shows you how to find the right place for you in your life and career—at any age!"

—**Brian Tracy,** author of *The Power of Self-Confidence*

"Kaufman gracefully infuses wisdom, insight, and practical advice to motivate and encourage people to pursue their dreams—no matter where they may be in their journey of life."

—**Sebastiano Tevarotto,** former corporate executive, current serial entrepreneur

"In the fast-paced world we live in today, you can easily find yourself 10, 20, 30 years into your career before realizing you are not where you thought you would be. Kristin Kaufman shares powerful stories to give people the courage to take a leap of faith, believe in themselves, and know they can transform their lives at any stage in life to realize their dreams."

—**Ed McLaughlin,** author of *The Purpose Is Profit*

"Kaufman's engrossing stories of success in the 'second half of life' is the inspiration we all need to take risks and pursue new experiences at every age."

—**Valerie Freeman,** Founder and CEO, Imprimis Group

"Since the creation of the public internet in the mid 1990s, global business has become increasingly driven by instant communication and eCommerce. As a result, it is has become easy to find yourself 10, 20, 30 years into your career questioning whether you are in the right job and are on the path to achieve the goals you created for yourself. Kaufman shares powerful stories of real people who took steps to realize their personal vision and goals. I believe this book gives people the courage to evaluate themselves and know they can transform their lives at any stage in life and still attain both success and happiness."

—**Tara Whitehead Stotland,**
Senior Vice-President, Aricent Group

"As someone with real life experience creating a second career later in life, Kristin Kaufman's *Is This Seat Taken? It's Never Too Late to Find the Right Seat* really spoke to me. It serves as inspiration for anyone who realizes a different path never taken. Her advice and wisdom are invaluable. I encourage anyone who seeks to shake up their professional life and make a change to read this book."

—**Bill Murphy,** CEO and Founder, Clos LaChance Wines

"Kaufman shares valuable and inspirational life lessons through the vibrant stories of men and women who achieved success in the 'second half' of life. Her practical advice provides readers with the confidence, drive, and ambition to persevere towards achieving an authentically successful life."

—**Shivaun M. Palmer,** CEO and
Co-Founder Plaid for Women, Inc.

"Kristin Kaufman's latest book reads as an owner's manual for life to those seeking wisdom and advice on how to finish strong."

—**Thomas Torkelson,** Founder
and CEO, IDEA Public Schools

"In the fast-paced world we live in today, you can easily find yourself 20-plus years into your career before realizing you are not where you thought you would be. Kaufman gives you a powerful set of stories about people who have found incredible success in this stage of their life. All of us can learn so much from people who have found success and who have faced some of the same questions we might have. Every story shouts out that hard work and perseverance to overcome a variety of tough odds is always rewarded with incredible life experiences."

—**Mark Hipp,** Operating Partner, Sterling Partners

"Having the pleasure of personally knowing Kristin Kaufman, I am continually inspired by her wisdom, experience and perspective on life. In her newest book, she has done a masterful job of putting in words, real life stories that can serve as an inspiration to anyone who is considering transforming their lives and venturing into new territories to achieve more meaningful life experiences."

—**Jim Sturm,** President and CEO, Brierley & Partners

"I also was inspired at age fifty to do something completely different from anything I'd done before, so Kaufman's stories really resonated with me."

—**Ellen Wood,** Co-Founder and CEO, The Teaching Trust

"Kristin Kaufman is a truth teller and a great story teller. If you are ready to learn, her message is the one you want to hear."

—**Katie Lazar,** Director of Sales &
Marketing, Cain Vineyard & Winery

"Using a factual short story approach and then providing personal insights and analysis Kaufman gives us a framework on how we should all approach this extended life that most baby boomers are now experiencing. We all have the opportunity to do it better, do it differently, or do whatever we have always dreamed of doing this second time around. We should all be inspired by this book and take full advantage of this opportunity."

—**David Sanders,** Founder, Dallas Advisory Partners

Is This Seat Taken?™

It's Never Too Late to Find the Right Seat

Kristin S. Kaufman

GREENLEAF
BOOK GROUP PRESS

Published by Greenleaf Book Group Press
Austin, Texas
www.gbgpress.com

Distributed by Greenleaf Book Group

For ordering information or special discounts for bulk purchases, please contact Greenleaf Book Group at PO Box 91869, Austin, TX 78709, 512.891.6100.

Design and composition by Greenleaf Book Group
Cover design by Greenleaf Book Group
Cover image: ©shutterstock.com/Lester Balajadia
Is This Seat Taken? is a registered trademark of Total Alignment, Inc.

Publisher's Cataloging-In-Publication Data

Kaufman, Kristin S.
  Is this seat taken? It's never too late to find the right seat / Kristin S. Kaufman.—
First edition.
    pages : illustrations ; cm
  Issued also as an ebook.
  Includes bibliographical references.
  ISBN: 978-1-62634-165-4
  1. Self-actualization (Psychology) 2. Self-realization in old age. 3. Choice (Psychology) 4. Life change events in old age. 5. Biography. I. Title.
II. Title: It's never too late to find the right seat
BF637.S4 K38 2015
158.1   2014945273

Part of the Tree Neutral® program, which offsets the number of trees consumed in the production and printing of this book by taking proactive steps, such as planting trees in direct proportion to the number of trees used: www.treeneutral.com

TreeNeutral®

Printed in the United States of America on acid-free paper

14 15 16 17 18 19   10 9 8 7 6 5 4 3 2 1

First Edition

For Gretchen, my treasured sister, friend,
and partner in life.

In memory of Ann Parsley Harper, my soul mate and editor of my first book, Is This Seat Taken? Random Encounters That Change Your Life.

Contents

Acknowledgments

I am grateful for a diverse, intelligent, and soulful circle of friends and colleagues who listen, encourage, and teach as we navigate life together. There are a few of you, and you know who you are, who have stood steadfastly by me over the past several years as I embarked on this entrepreneurial and creative venture. You will never know how grateful I am to you and for you.

Thank you to my sister and partner through life, Gretchen, to whom I dedicate this book. She challenges and supports in equal measure and helps me grow into the person I can become. She is the best sister anyone could want. I express infinite gratitude to my parents for who they are, and for all they have done and continue to do in their lives. They are my teachers and role models in every aspect of life. The love our family shares is boundless and I thank God daily for it. The foundation of faith and love, on which our parents steadied our family, is our bedrock. My parents and sister are the greatest blessings in my life.

Thank you to my attorney and friend, Gary Solomon, for his expert advice, voice of reason, and patient support. Thank you to Jennifer Brokaw for her steadfastness in supporting me and the growth of my businesses. Thank you to the talented team at Greenleaf Book Group, led by Justin Branch, who said 'yes' to me and to this project, and subsequently showed me what a good experience in book publishing feels like. Thank you to Brandy Savarese, editor at Greenleaf Book Group, for embracing this project with quiet confidence and professionalism.

Finally, this book would not have come to fruition without the support, encouragement, and guidance of my friend and editor Ann Parsley Harper. Ann and I forged a soul mate connection during the creation of *Is This Seat Taken? Random Encounters That Change Your Life*. Her partnership in the conception and development of *Is This Seat Taken? It's Never Too Late to Find the Right Seat* was invaluable. Ann lost her courageous battle with cancer as the final manuscript was being submitted. Her wisdom and compassion were integral to this accomplishment, which I am grateful to have experienced. Her smile and her voice will be in my heart always.

Author's Note

The idea for this book has been percolating for more than ten years. It comes from the harsh realization that many are finding themselves in a position in life not planned, not expected, and not desired, and they are in a quandary. Their resounding question is: "Now, *what* am I going to do?!"

How many times have you asked this question of yourself, of those closest to you, or to no one in particular, just in an exasperated cry to the universe? Over the course of my life, and particularly in my current profession, I have heard this phrase countless times. You may feel that you have made poor choices, that your opportunities have passed you by, or that the music has stopped, as if you are playing musical chairs, and all the seats were indeed taken.

I dare say, there is not a single human being who at least once in his or her life has not faced an unforeseen situation, a newfound reality, a daunting challenge, or a veiled opportunity, and not wondered what to do.

This book is geared toward those individuals who have come to a fork in the road, taken a path, and found themselves twenty to thirty (or more) years later in a place they didn't quite recognize. The dilemma is relevant for anyone, at any age, at any station in life, who wakes up and is not sure what they are going to do next or how to move forward. In some cases the dilemma may simply be that they need to figure out how to re-tap the chutzpah to keep on going.

Let's face it. The world is and will continue to be a very different place than many of us experienced growing up. The realities of what many are facing are far from the *Leave It to Beaver* and *I Love Lucy* images on which we were reared. The simplicities of Frank Capra's *It's A Wonderful Life* can seem far and distant from the complexities of global competitiveness, social media convergence, and real-time transparency in virtually every aspect of our lives, and the increasing financial pressures for the basic necessities of healthcare, education, and a comfortable standard of living.

Between now and 2050, the world's population is expected to grow by approximately 2.3 billion people, eventually reaching more than 9 billion. In the United States alone, the population is projected to be over 450 million. It is startling to realize that the number of us over sixty-five is expected to *more than double* between 2012 and 2060, from 43 million to 92 million. And relative to the baby boomers, the 77 million of us born between 1946 and 1964, this number will grow to 2.4 million.

That is a daily statistic of 12,500 people turning fifty each day—or one every seven seconds! This aging population will certainly place a burden on society as a whole; yet, more specifically, each of us will feel the pinch personally. There are numerous books, studies, and blogs that tout the plight of the economy, the growth of the aging population, and the side effects these realities will have on every generation from this point forward.

The world as we once knew it is over. Recent graduates are out of work, are finding it very hard to find a job, and are often forced to live at home with their parents. Those in their thirties and forties are struggling to buy their first homes and to determine if they can even afford to have a family. And then there are those of us in our fifties and sixties who are not yet eligible for Medicare or Social Security (even though there may not be much to go around when our time comes anyway). The raw reality that the average income today is significantly below what it was prior to the most recent economic crisis of 2007. In addition, this particularly unfortunate segment of our population often finds itself pinched between housing college-graduate children and taking care of aging parents. It is easy, and actually quite prevalent, in many circles to become disenchanted and discouraged with these new realities and practicalities of life as we know them today.

Yes, there are those fortunate enough to find themselves in the top 1 percent income bracket. On average, this small percentage will bring in an annual gross income of more than $350,000. And there are others who have made it into the very *top* 1 percent of *net worth* individuals, who have—by most studies—amassed more than $8.4 million, or sixty-nine times the average household's assets. So, yes, there are those who do not—and probably will never—feel the money pinch and this new definition of a mid-life crisis; yet, they may be having other epiphanies relative to their lives. For this elite group, this book will still give pause, as many of these true stories will show. Though financial security is a necessity and they may have this particular aspect covered, as we know, it is not the only ingredient for a fulfilling life. Simply stated: money is not the only metric.

There have always been, and always will be, challenges in life. The impediments have differed for every generation. We most certainly do not have the corner on that market. Many of us remember our parents and grandparents sharing the hardships brought courtesy of the Great Depression. This complete reset of life as we knew it started in the United States in 1929, and became worldwide news when the stock market crashed. No one was left unscathed. Personal savings were wiped out; it had devastating effects around the world, in both rich and poor countries. Personal income disintegrated and domestic prices and profits dropped, while international trade plunged by more than 50 percent. Unemployment in the United States rose to 25 percent and in some countries rose as high as 33 percent. So, the times we are facing today are not unprecedented.

Over the years, I have met folks from all walks of life, from successful senior-level business executives, board members of publicly traded entities, and real estate tycoons, to trust-fund babies and self-made millionaires. Many of these people, though financially wealthy, are disillusioned, dissatisfied, and still seeking that ever elusive sense of being fully whole.

And, more prevalently of late, I am meeting countless men and women who are of an age when they thought they would be retired, playing golf in a gated community, leading a foundation built from their own accumulation of wealth, or building orphanages or schools in an underprivileged region of the world. They never fathomed they would be unemployed, with not enough left of their investments, and wondering how they were going to live for the next thirty years (or longer) in the manner in which they had become accustomed. They are distraught. They wonder if their dreams will always remain dreams. They wonder how they will provide for themselves in a world where age discrimination in the workplace is rampant.

I believe we have lessons we are to learn and to teach while we are here. I call this earth school. Each experience is different, each story is unique, and each manner of contribution perfect in the way it is revealed and manifested. This particular book was written to give hope, inspiration, and applicable lessons as derived from the lives of men and women who found new and unexpected success—by many definitions—late in life. These are stories of notable individuals as well as those not known by the general public. Over the course of history, there have been countless stories of the so-called late bloomers, those who through serendipity, necessity, desire, and Divine providence created legacies completely unpredictable in their early life. In fact, for each individual's story, the catalytic event that placed them on their trajectory of boundless opportunity did not occur in most cases until sometime after they had turned fifty.

As diverse as their stories are, the common characteristic of their transformation is that it began late in life. Their lives took on new and exciting changes, which affected their personal legacies as well as the many lives they touched along the way. Many prospered monetarily, while others made tremendous contributions artistically. The core tenets of their individual life lessons are the golden nuggets, which we will explore for application in our own lives.

Finally, each of these individuals aligned with their purpose. Our power as individuals fully manifests when we become authentically aligned. As I explored in my first book, *Is This Seat Taken? Random Encounters That Change Your Life,* my definition of alignment is when we learn and embrace what we love to do, we are good at it, and it is tied to something greater than ourselves. Self-awareness is the key to revealing our most ideal state of alignment. At the end of the book, you'll find summaries of a few key observations that will help you see beyond your own limiting beliefs and societal expectations so that you can unleash your personal potential and become fully aligned—whatever your age, socioeconomic station, or predisposition to your past or your future.

One critical point to remember: the people featured in this book are just folks, like you and me. They are not superheroes. They were not privileged by way of education, financial bounty, or fame prior to their mid- to late-life resurgence. They came from extremely diverse and, in all cases, humble backgrounds. Yet there are salient synergies in their value systems and how they met and approached their challenges and opportunities.

Thus, my intention for this book is to give a giant B-12 shot of encouragement and guidance, anchored by real-life stories, to each reader. Despite the unfolding conditions in our world today and the increasing pressures of how these realities will affect each of us, it is never too late to make the contribution we were placed on the earth to make and to build the life we want. It is never too late to chase your dreams. Remember, *you* own the outcome. No one else does. My hope is that these remarkable stories will light a spark—whether you are twenty-five or sixty-five—to take back the reins of your life and become clear on exactly what you are going to do *now* and how you wish to contribute to the world. The music has not stopped, and there is still time to find your seat.

Tell me, what is it you plan to do with your
one wild and precious life?
—Mary Oliver

Laura Ingalls Wilder
Published Destiny

It is the sweet, simple things of life
which are the real ones after all.
—Laura Ingalls Wilder

Most of us know of Laura Ingalls Wilder through her best-selling series of books, which chronicled her pioneering childhood in the late 1800s. The books were so well loved that they were ultimately made into the television series *Little House on the Prairie*, which was a staple in most households from 1974 to 1982. What you may not know is that Laura's life was not always the charmed childhood depicted by actor Melissa Gilbert.

Her seemingly idyllic life began in 1867, in a rural area of Wisconsin, where her first book *Little House in the Big Woods* was centered. In her early childhood, her father, Charles

Ingalls, settled in Indian Territory, on land not yet open for homesteading. This experience formed the basis for the *Little House* series. In the subsequent years of Laura's childhood, her father's restless spirit led them on various moves. From Wisconsin, they moved to Walnut Grove, Minnesota, and then to Burr Oak, Iowa. In 1879, Charles Ingalls accepted a railroad job, which took him to the eastern Dakota Territory, where he and his wife, Caroline, resided for the rest of their lives. There the Ingalls family watched the town of De Smet literally rise up from the prairie.

Once the family was settled, Laura was enrolled in school, worked several part-time jobs, and made many friends. Two months before her sixteenth birthday, Laura accepted her first professional position, teaching three terms in a one-room schoolhouse. She did not particularly enjoy teaching, but from a very young age, she felt a responsibility to help her family financially. As one can imagine, wage-earning opportunities for women in those days were limited. She not only taught school but also worked for the local dressmaker and continued her own studies in high school.

When she was eighteen, Laura met and fell in love with Almanzo Wilder, a bachelor pioneer, who was ten years her senior. At this point, she stopped teaching school and continuing her own studies. This was a pivotal juncture, as she never graduated from high school. They married and achieved great prosperity on their homestead claim. Their prospects seemed bright. They moved to a new home just north of De Smet, and began their life together. A year later, she gave birth to their first child, Rose.

Though their married life began with great promise, the first few years came with many trials. Almanzo became partially paralyzed from a life-threatening bout of diphtheria. He eventually regained nearly full use of his legs, but he needed a cane to walk for the remainder of his life. This setback, among many others, began a series of disastrous events that included the death of their unnamed newborn son, the destruction of their home and barn by fire, and several years of severe drought that left them in debt, physically ill, and unable to earn a living from their 320 acres of prairie land. Many of these trials were chronicled in Laura's manuscript, *The First Four Years*, which was discovered and published in the early 1970s, after Rose's death.

In 1890, Laura and Almanzo left De Smet and spent time resting at his parents' farm in Minnesota before ultimately deciding to move to Florida. They sought Florida's climate for health reasons, yet they were both used to living on the dry plains and ultimately wilted in the heat and humidity. After a very short time, they returned to De Smet, rented a small house, and began to rebuild their lives. Almanzo became a day laborer and Laura became a seamstress at a local dressmaker's shop. Their hope was to earn and save enough money to once again start a farm.

A few years later, the hard-pressed and financially strapped young couple moved to Mansfield, Missouri, using their hard-earned savings to make a down payment on a piece of undeveloped property just outside of town. They named their homestead Rocky Ridge Farm. It consisted of forty acres and a windowless, ramshackle log cabin. The couple's climb to financial security was a slow process. Initially, their only income came from wagonloads of firewood that Almanzo sold for 50 cents in town, the result of the backbreaking work of clearing the trees and stones from their land. The apple trees they planted did not bear fruit for seven years. Barely able to eke out more than a subsistence living on the new farm, the Wilders were forced to move into nearby Mansfield, where they rented a small house. Almanzo found work as an oil sales-man and general delivery man, while Laura took in boarders and served meals to local railroad workers. Their future was uncertain on many levels.

Not too long after the move, Almanzo's parents paid their daughter-in-law and son a visit and surprised them with the deed to the Mansfield house they had been renting. This was the economic jumpstart the young couple needed. They sold their house in town and used the proceeds from the sale to complete Rocky Ridge Farm. They moved back to the farm per-manently. What began as about forty acres of thickly wooded, stone-covered hillside with a small log cabin evolved into a two-hundred-acre, relatively prosperous, diversified poultry, dairy, and fruit farm and an impressive ten-room farmhouse.

The Wilders were active in various regional farm asso-ciations, and they were greatly respected as authorities in poultry farming and rural living. This recognition led to invi-tations to speak and share their knowledge to various groups around the region. They had achieved a great level of success, by many measures.

Around this time, Laura became inspired by her daughter's budding writing career and began to write herself. In 1911, an invitation to submit an article to the *Missouri Ruralist* led Laura to accept a permanent position as a columnist and editor with that publication. She also took a paid position with a Farm Loan Association, dispensing small loans to local farmers from her office in the farmhouse. These additional sources of revenue helped the Wilders to build up savings and to continue enhancing their farm and the surrounding areas.

Her column in the *Missouri Ruralist*, "As a Farm Woman Thinks," soon had a loyal audience. Her topics ranged from home and family to world events and Rose's fascinating world travels, and her own thoughts on the increasing options offered to women during the era. While the Wilders were not wealthy at this stage in their lives, the farming operation and Laura's additional income from writing and the Farm Loan Association provided a stable enough living for them to finally place themselves in Mansfield's middle-class society. Laura's social circle consisted of the wives of wealthy business owners, doctors, and lawyers, and her social club activities took up much of her time.

During this period, Rose heavily encouraged her mother to develop a more notable writing career for national magazines, as she herself had quite successfully accomplished. For some reason, Laura was unable or unwilling to make the leap from writing for these smaller publications to the higher-paying national market.

By the 1920s, after decades of prosperity, Laura and Almanzo began to simplify their lives. They made the decision to scale back the farming operation considerably and Laura resigned from her positions with the *Missouri Ruralist* and the

Farm Loan Association. They hired outside help to take care of the farm work that Almanzo, now in his seventies, could no longer easily manage. A comfortable and worry-free retirement seemed probable for the Wilders as they settled into the golden years of their lives.

Tragically, in 1929, the stock market crash wiped out the majority of their investment portfolio. Though they still owned their home and the two hundred acres on which it resided, they had invested most of their savings in the stock market. Though they had faced many hardships throughout their time together, the reality that decades of grueling work and hard-won savings had evaporated overnight was likely hard to grasp. Their dream of a worry-free and financially stable retirement had been snuffed out in an instant. They became dependent upon Rose as their primary means of financial support, a position they never dreamed they would face.

Losing their life savings, together with the deaths of Laura's beloved mother, Caroline, and sister, Mary, within a three-year period seemed to have prompted Laura to preserve her memories in a life story she called *Pioneer Girl*. She hoped that her writing would generate additional income and help her to reclaim their financial independence. She solicited Rose's opinion on her writing, as Rose had achieved moderate prominence in literary circles. With Rose's encouragement and facilitation of publishing connections, *Little House in the Big Woods* was published by Harper and Brothers in 1932. Laura was sixty-four years old.

The initial release was quite successful, so Laura continued to create the series about herself, her family, and their experiences. Her last book, *These Happy Golden Years*, was released in 1943, when she was seventy-six years old. The writing and ongoing collaboration with Rose brought national acclaim and the money the Wilders needed to recoup the loss of their investments in the stock market.

Since the publication of *Little House in the Big Woods* in 1931, the books have been continually in print and have been translated into forty languages. Laura's first—and smallest—royalty check from Harper and Brothers in 1932 was for $500, which is the equivalent of approximately $11,000 in 2014 dollars. By the mid-1930s the royalties from the Little House books brought a steady and increasingly substantial income to the Wilders for the first time in their fifty years of marriage. Various honors, huge amounts of fan mail, and other accolades were granted to Laura Ingalls Wilder in the last twenty years of her life.

During their final years together, Laura and Almanzo were frequently alone at Rocky Ridge Farm. Most of the surrounding land had been sold off, but they still kept a few farm animals, and they tended their flower beds and vegetable gardens. Almost daily, carloads of fans would stop by, eager to meet "Laura" of the Little House books. She and Almanzo lived independently and without financial worries until Almanzo's death in 1949, at the age of ninety-two. Though Laura grieved, she was determined to remain independent and stay on the farm, despite her daughter's constant requests that her mother come live with her permanently in Connecticut. For the next eight years, Laura lived alone. She was a familiar figure in Mansfield, being brought into town regularly by her driver to run errands, attend church, or visit friends. She continued an active correspondence with her editors, many fans, and friends during these final years.

Laura had an extremely competitive spirit going all the way back to the schoolyard as a child, and she had remarked to many people that she wanted to live to be ninety, "because Almanzo had." She succeeded. Laura died in her sleep at her Mansfield farmhouse on February 10, 1957, three days after her ninetieth birthday.

The Laura Ingalls Wilder beloved by generations left a literary legacy all written after she'd turned sixty-four.

Finding Creativity through Crisis

As a child, Laura Ingalls Wilder was by far my favorite author. Though, I also gravitated to the Nancy Drew mysteries and to the adventures of Pippi Longstocking, there was something about the Big Woods, the Ingalls family, and all the eccentric characters in the *Little House* books that resonated with me. It never occurred to me that Laura Ingalls Wilder wrote those books when she was an elderly woman. In fact, I am quite sure I thought she had written them as a young girl, when she was about my age. It was startling to realize during my research just how late in life she began what would become her legacy-defining collection.

Laura Ingalls Wilder's journey is laden with lessons. A

resilient spirit in those days was as common as blood and sweat. Government subsidy programs were nonexistent, and the abundance of wealth from which charitable contributions could come was scarce. Thus, when faced with an adversity such as your barn and all your worldly possessions burning to the ground, stalwart strength was expected and honored. There was no time for self-pity or petty envy of another's riches. Her scrappy resolve to plow through each hurdle is humbling. She and Almanzo carved a life out of dust on the prairie and then virtually lost it all at a time in which they thought they would retire. Yet, soldier on they did.

It has been said that necessity is the mother of invention. The impetus for the *Little House* books was in response to Laura's stark reality of needing to generate income for their retirement. Despite her daughter's interest and encouragement to extend her writing beyond regional publications in previous years, it wasn't until she faced devastating financial hardship that Laura swallowed her fears and insecurities and created what would become her ultimate legacy.

Laura's childhood laid the foundational values that sustained her throughout the rest of her life. The family's hardships, heartaches, loves, and losses were the seeds from which her literary garden grew. As a child and young adult, it is doubtful she ever thought or even dreamed that one day the recollection of her experiences would make her famous and a treasured icon in children's literature. This is one of the greatest lessons her life teaches us. One never knows what the future holds and how the daily repetitive rhythms of life may inform how you ultimately contribute to the world. Our lives are a compilation of moments and memories, and our destiny is most certainly what we choose to create from those experiences. Laura wrote about her childhood and transfixed generations of young girls and boys. In doing so, she wrote her own final chapter, which extended far beyond the Big Woods in which it began.

Alignment Lessons: Make It Real

- Tragedies and hardships are part of life; it is how we confront them that seals our fate.

- Our destiny is what we ultimately create.

- We are a compilation of all the experiences in our life; each one teaches us something new.

- Face your fears, as they can light ways to new experiences and opportunities.

The real things haven't changed. It is still
best to be honest and truthful;
to make the most of what we have; to be
happy with simple pleasures;
and have courage when things go wrong.
—Laura Ingalls Wilder

Anna Mary Robertson
Grandma Moses

I look back on my life like a good day's work; it was done and I feel satisfied with it. I was happy and contented, I knew nothing better and made the best out of what life offered. And life is what we make it, always has been, always will be.
—**Grandma Moses,** as quoted in
My Life's History, 1951

Anna Mary Robertson had lived eighty-seven years before her life took a dramatic and totally unexpected twist. Eighty-seven years full of joy, sadness, depression, ambiguity, and death. No one could have ever predicted her life would evolve in the manner in which it did.

Anna Mary was born in a small rural community in upstate

New York in 1860. She was one of ten children reared in a close-knit family. She had a very close relationship with her father in particular. He was a simple man who loved to take long walks in the woods around their humble home and who viewed the world through a pure and simple lens. His devotion to the outdoors and respect for the natural order of things was his moral and spiritual compass. This was the code in which he reared his family, and this belief system became foundational to Anna Mary and her siblings.

Anna Mary and her nine brothers and sisters were not afraid of hard work. Her five brothers helped with the family farm, and she and her four sisters were taught basic homemaking and domestic skills. They lived a sparse life enriched by the pleasure of simple things, like the morning calls of the mockingbird and the full fireball of the burnt-orange sunset. They wanted for nothing, as they could never miss what they never had.

At only twelve years of age, Anna Mary left the comfort and love of her family to work as what was referred to as a "hired girl" on a neighboring farm. She became a housekeeper and helped a wealthier family with their household chores. What little formal education she received was acquired in a one-room schoolhouse not far from the farm on which she worked. There was little time for fun, frivolity, or outside exposure. She worked as a housekeeper on this farm for more than fifteen years, remaining single, which in that time would have labeled her an old maid.

Miraculously, when she was twenty-seven, a young, strapping man was hired on as a houseboy on the same farm. His name was Thomas Moses. Anna Mary and Thomas courted briefly and fell in love. In 1887, just a few months after meeting, they were married.

The newlyweds believed that the Reconstruction-era South was to be a land of opportunity. Within hours of their wedding, the couple boarded a train bound for North Carolina, where Thomas had secured a job managing a horse ranch. They didn't make it; they stopped in Staunton, Virginia, to spend the night, and they never left. While there, they were approached to take over as tenants on a local farm. Wanting a new beginning and eager to set down roots, they decided to invest their mere $600 in the rental of this farm. Anna Mary immediately fell in love with the beautiful Shenandoah Valley, and they made it their home for more than twenty years. Anna Mary is remembered as saying that her "chilly New York State home—albeit mountainous—would forever after seem a swamp by comparison."

In their early years of marriage, times were very tough. Anna Mary had always been a hard worker and believed in pulling her weight. Scrappy by nature, she bought a cow with her own savings, churned butter, and also made potato chips to sell to her neighbors for extra money. Her resolve was steadfast. Despite these trying times, she was always known to be "cheerful as a cricket." Through the course of their life together, Anna Mary and Thomas had ten children. Sadly, they buried five of them before they reached their first birthdays. Despite these formidable circumstances, Anna Mary was sturdy and a dutiful farmer's wife and mother. She never was one to bathe in self-pity or focus on their lack of material wealth. They continued to persevere and focus on the matters at hand. Through those years of diligent, disciplined work, her family prospered, eventually earning enough to buy their own farm.

It was during this time that her neighbors christened her "Mother Moses," for her loving actions and neighborly manner. She loved Virginia and happily would have spent the rest of her life there. However, Thomas was homesick for New York. In 1905 they bought a farm in Eagle Bridge, New York, not far from where she was born. She used to say, "Not one thing has changed since we left; the gates are hanging on one hinge since I went away." They named their new farm Mount Nebo after the biblical mountain where Moses disappeared. She and Thomas lived a quiet life for more than two decades, rearing their remaining children and working the long hours of a rural farm.

When Thomas died twenty-two years later, Anna Moses, at the spry age of sixty-seven, had no choice but to take the helm in operating their farm, with the help of her sons, to provide for herself and her family. It was in the depths of the Depression, and they had no other option.

Not too many years after Thomas's death, Anna Mary received an urgent call from her daughter Anna, who was suffering from tuberculosis. She moved to Vermont to be with her daughter, and became her primary caretaker during her illness. During this time, Anna showed her mother a picture that had been embroidered in yarn, and she challenged her mother to duplicate it.

It was there, at her daughter's home, that a creative spark was lit within Anna Mary. She began stitching what she called "worsted" pictures—worsted being a type of yarn used in embroidery work—and giving them away to anyone who would take them. These pieces were reminiscent of country farm life, resembling Currier and Ives prints. She called upon her lifetime of memories of her own mother and father, the walks in the woods, and the many decades of farm life as muses for her creations.

Life dealt another blow when Anna succumbed to tuberculosis, leaving Anna Mary to care for her grandchildren. Now in her seventies, Anna Mary became a mother again to two young children. As with all things in her life, she took this responsibility in stride and played the hand she was dealt with grace and fortitude.

Anna Mary continued to create these whimsical embroidered pieces until one day, when she was attempting to thread rich-colored wool yarn through the elusive eye of the tiny needle she used, she grimaced from the pain in her arthritic hands. After numerous failed attempts, she sighed deeply and silently surrendered. As she examined the half-stitched embroidered farm scene, her fingers, crippled from seventy-two years of life, throbbed from the effort. When she complained that her hands made it hard for her to hold a needle, her sister Celestia suggested she take up painting instead. It was in this casual "invention out of necessity" manner, at the age of seventy-five, in which the final, legacy-building chapter in Anna Mary's life would begin to unfold.

Anna Mary loathed being idle. Before too long, she had accumulated a large collection of paintings. She would take these initial works of art and her canned fruits and jams to the local crafts fairs in the area. Ironically, the jams won a blue ribbon and her paintings came back home with her. During this period, her career might have been snuffed out had she not been a sensible woman. From her perspective, to pursue art for art's sake alone would be sheer folly and indulgence.

As fate would have it, the wife of a druggist in the neighboring village of Hoosick Falls invited Anna Mary to contribute a few of her paintings to a women's exchange she was organizing. For several years, those paintings, along with crafts and other objects created by local homemakers, gathered dust in the drugstore window. During Easter week of 1938, a New York City collector named Louis Caldor happened to come through town. Mr. Caldor traveled regularly in connection with his job as an engineer for the New York City water department. He had a hobby of seeking out native artistic "finds." The paintings in the drugstore window caught his eye, and he asked to see more. He ended up buying the whole lot. He also got Anna Mary's name and address and set off to meet her in person. With this meeting, Anna Mary's life changed.

The beautiful irony of this story is that Anna Mary created all her paintings from memory. She once said, "I will sit quietly and remember and imagine. Then I'll get an inspiration and start painting. Then I will forget everything except how things used to be and how to paint it so that people will know how we used to live."

For Anna Mary, the ability to sit, remember, and recall her life's story was the magic alchemy creating her next chapter. She would perch on two large pillows atop an old, battered swivel chair. There was no easel. The Masonite on which she painted would lie flat on the kitchen table. From meager, humble surroundings came her authentic reflection of her life.

Anna Mary Robertson Moses, or Grandma Moses as she became known, lived a very hard life. She buried her parents, all her siblings, her husband, and every one of her children before she died, at age 101. She had scraped and struggled, living a simple, rural life through the Depression, until the ripe age of seventy-nine, when her life began to change. Despite her success as a folk artist, her value system remained simple and offers today's generation thoughts to ponder:

> Now that I am ninety-five years old, looking back over the years, I have seen many changes taking place. So many inventions have been made. Things now go faster. In olden times, things were not so rushed. I think people were more content, more satisfied with life than they are today. You don't hear nearly as much laughter and shouting as you did in my day, and what was fun for us wouldn't be fun now . . . In this age I don't think people are as happy; they are worried. They're too anxious to get ahead of their neighbors; they are striving and striving to get something better. I do think in a way that they have too much now. We did with much less.

Throughout her 101 years, she found joy and delight sharing her creations—whether it was butter, jam, embroidered cloths, or her paintings. Each represented a reflection of the life she adored.

Despite her advanced years, in the last few decades of her life, she painted more than a thousand paintings, twenty-five of these after her hundredth birthday. These paintings, which initially could be bought for a mere $3 to $5, were later sold for $8,000 to $10,000. They are now valued into the millions. The amount of money she accumulated by the end of her life pales compared to the other aspects of her life's contribution.

Grandma Moses's artistic legacy was created and built in the last twenty years of her life.

Abundance through Simplicity

My first exposure to Grandma Moses was when I was a little girl. My family received a Christmas card that depicted a wintry scene with horse-drawn sleighs, a snowy game of tag, and country life under snow-laden trees. It was a nostalgic panorama of a slower-paced life and finding pleasure through simple things. It was alluring and drew me into the make-believe lives of the miniature people scattered on the hillside. I did not know Grandma Moses's entire story until decades later. I now know that the distinct simplicity with which she viewed and painted her world is in direct alignment with who she was.

It is humbling to realize that Anna Mary Robertson Moses did not have wealth, prestige, or advanced education through more than the first eighty years of her life. Simplicity was the music to which her heart sang. She found richness in the morning bird's call and the sweetness in homemade peach jam from the orchard's first harvest. Grandma Moses's distinction was her innate appreciation for the sanctity of modest living, which manifested in her life and art. Her ability to embrace the grace of everyday beauty and wonder and translate this into her art was her gift to this world.

The painter Anna Mary became was a product of many serendipitous happenings. Her career was never contrived, strategized, or methodically masterminded. As with most things in life, her direction was steered by a series of occurrences, which I choose to believe are the hands of Divine Providence. Had her only surviving daughter not had tuberculosis, she would not have moved to Vermont to take care of her. Had she not had severe arthritis, she might never have given up needlework nor picked up the bulkier paintbrush, which she could nestle between her swollen knuckles. Had an engineer with a propensity for local artists not walked down a rural main street in the spring of 1938, her paintings might never have been discovered. All these incidental occurrences happened very late in her life, with no premeditation on her part. Yet, and most inspiring, at age eighty-seven, she was open to the unfamiliar fresh breeze that blew into her life that year. To use a common phrase of our times, she *leaned in* and clutched the opportunity that was presented to her. There were no expectations, no set directions, and no demands from Grandma Moses for a new journey. She allowed her talented preparation to take hold of the opportunity.

What a paradoxical lesson she has taught us with her courage. Through her ability to charmingly depict the beauty of an innocent and uncomplicated life through her paintings, she created a charmed final act for her life.

Alignment Lessons: Make It Real

- There is beauty all around you.

- You must remain present in the moment, as the greatest opportunity may be right before your eyes.

- Awaken to what is around you – this is where there is magic.

- Riches lie in the simplest of details.

- Many years can pass before a fork in the road appears.

I look out the window sometimes to seek the color of the shadows and the different greens in the trees, but when I get ready to paint I just close my eyes and imagine a scene.
—Grandma Moses

Harland Sanders
Kentucky's Unlikely Colonel

*I made a resolve then that I was going to
amount to something if I could. And no
hours, nor amount of labor, nor amount
of money would deter me from giving
the best that there was in me. And I have
done that ever since, and I win by it.*
—Harland Sanders

Harland Sanders's life was riddled with adversity from the day he was born. He came into the world in a four-room shack on a country road in rural Indiana in the fall of 1890. At the tender age of six, his father died suddenly, forcing his mother to work in a tomato-canning factory nearby. The oldest of the three children, Harland was responsible for taking care of his younger sisters and cooking for the family.

This serendipitous domestic responsibility was Providence, as it would plant the seeds that would ultimately shape his life going forward.

When Harland was twelve, he had to drop out of school with only a sixth-grade education to provide for the family. He held many odd jobs in his early life. He was a farmhand, an army-mule tender, a locomotive fireman, a railroad worker, an insurance salesman, a ferryboat entrepreneur, and a tire salesman. He was even an amateur obstetrician, and had the opportunity to deliver babies in the rural mountain communities. Harland's life was a series of hairpin curves. He was regularly in and out of work, as were many during this economic period.

In the mid-1920s, an unemployed Harland was hitchhiking to Louisville, Kentucky, in search of a job. As he was heading back home to Winchester, a man in a large Cadillac picked him up. It turned out this man was the general manager of Standard Oil Company of Kentucky. During the course of the conversation, the man asked Harland if he thought he could run a service station. Harlan's simple response was, "I can do anything anyone else can do." It was that meeting that gave Harland the initial break he needed.

The service station in Nicholasville, Kentucky, was not doing very well and was in need of a new operator. Harland was their man. This was the first time in his life that he felt he had control over his own destiny. Up until this point, he had been in large part dependent upon others for his future. At the service station, Harlan sold gas for fifteen cents a gallon, earning two cents' profit on each gallon, and sold ethyl for nineteen cents, on which he made four cents' profit. The first day he only sold three-and-a-half gallons of gas, altogether.

The station was located on a corner, and the traffic was constant, so the opportunity was there. Honing his customer-service skills, in addition to pumping gas, Harland began to fill radiators, wash windshields, and brush the mud off the floorboards. No one was offering customer service like this. As Harland once said, "This was service for nothing." His extra efforts began to pay off for him in huge dividends. Within weeks, he was selling 15,000-18,000 gallons of gas each month. He continued to add services for his customers, from changing and replacing flat tires to opening at 5 a.m. to catch the early commuters. This business was his first real success, and lasted for many years. The Depression of 1929 and a drought in the heavily agriculturally oriented region ultimately put him out of business. Harland Sanders was busted. Bankrupt. He was forty years old.

His personal life was equally tumultuous. Up to this point, he had married, divorced, married again, and had three children. His only son, Harland Junior, died at age twenty due to complications from blood poisoning contracted from a routine tonsillectomy. His life was certainly not peaceful or easy by any standard. He had had more than his fair share of tragedy and misfortune.

Due to the success of his service station in Nicholasville, Shell Oil Company offered to build a service station for him in Corbin, Kentucky, in 1930. It was here that Harland, in the same spirit of offering more service than gasoline, began cooking for hungry travelers who stopped in to buy gasoline. His patrons dined at his kitchen table in the station's humble living quarters. It was in this unassuming canteen that he invented what became known as the "home meal replacement," which translated into selling "complete meals to busy, time-strapped families." He called it, "Sunday Dinner, Seven Days a Week." Before long, this diner became the spot at which to eat in this area of Kentucky, serving country ham, chicken dishes, and soul food. It was open twenty-four hours a day. Harland was quoted to say, "You can sleep a man only once in twenty-four hours, but you can feed him three times." This simple observation helped Harland realize that his future resided in the food service industry.

As Harland's fame grew, Governor Ruby Laffoon made him a Kentucky Colonel in 1935 in recognition of his contributions to the state's cuisine. In 1939, the food critic Duncan Hines visited the restaurant incognito and was so impressed that he listed the place in his *Adventures in Good Eating*. This was just four years after Harland had opened the restaurant, and the listing proved to be an enormous boon for his business, much as a Zagat's or Fodor's five-star rating would be today.

As more people started coming strictly for the food, Harland moved the restaurant across the street to increase its capacity. His business expanded to 124 seats and an adjacent motel. Over the next decade, he built a thriving, reputable business and perfected his secret blend of eleven herbs and spices and his pressure cooker technique for frying chicken—preserving tender juicy meat while making the outside crunchy.

Then the entire trajectory of his business and his life changed again. During President Eisenhower's administration, the great road-building program known as the Interstate Highway

System was launched throughout the nation. This announcement meant that the new Interstate Route 75 would replace the old US Route 25, and this new interstate would bypass the city of Corbin altogether. Harland knew he had to sell his business, as his experience had taught him that success for a service station and other tourist services was entirely dependent upon location. He ended up auctioning off the restaurant and the motel—which represented twenty years of his life—for a mere $75,000. He had been forced to sell the small business he had poured his heart and soul into over the past 20 years, all because an interstate highway now bypassed the small town of Corbin, Kentucky. At sixty-five years old, he was barely able to pay his outstanding bills and taxes with the proceeds. He had virtually nothing left. His only source of income for his family was a meager monthly Social Security check of $105.

The year was 1955. Confident of the quality of his fried chicken, Harland Sanders then devoted himself to starting over from scratch, with nothing but his chicken recipe, his hard-earned experience, and his discipline to work hard. He began to build a franchise business for frying chicken. He was dirt poor again and was literally going door to door to sell his concept. At first, he tried to sell to the large, reputable, prestigious restaurants. This approach was not as successful as he had hoped. More than one snubbed him and his approach to country fare. Many nights, he would return to his car to sleep, unbeknownst to his prospective partners.

Then, a second serendipitous meeting would change the direction of his business. Harland met Pete Harman at a National Restaurant Association meeting in Chicago. Both men had operated small restaurants, Harland in Corbin, Kentucky, and Pete in Salt Lake City, Utah. Harland had wanted Pete to try his fried chicken, noting that all small restaurants want a signature dish for which they are known and that competitors don't have. Pete was reluctant. Finally, Harland convinced him to let him cook some chicken for him. It was the first time Harland had done this outside of his restaurant. After scrounging up a pressure cooker and frying up a chicken with all the fixin's, Harland and Pete sat down to eat. They devoured every morsel. Pete decided to feature Harland's Kentucky Fried Chicken in his restaurant, which became the first big showplace for other potential franchises.

Harland pounded the pavement with his cooking gear, broilers, and spice recipe for weeks at a time. He said that the one thing that kept him going was the conviction that his chicken was good and that it would be good for the restaurant owner and good for the customers who ate it. He later attributed this unwavering conviction to his service in Rotary International, where he'd been introduced to the Four Way Test, the foundation for Rotary: "Is it the truth? Is it fair to all concerned? Will it build goodwill and better friendships? Will it be beneficial to all concerned?" He was a member of Rotary for more than fifty-six years, and as long as his business could abide by these rules, he knew he would make it.

Fewer than ten years later, Harland Sanders had more than six hundred Kentucky Fried Chicken franchises in the United States and Canada. In 1964, he sold his interest in the United States company for $2 million to a group of investors, including John Y. Brown, Jr., who later became the governor of Kentucky.

Until he was fatally stricken with leukemia in 1980 at the age of ninety, the Colonel traveled 250,000 miles a year, visiting KFC restaurants around the world. His likeness continues to appear on millions of buckets of his unique chicken and on thousands of restaurants in more than one hundred countries around the world. The overall financial value of the KFC enterprise exceeds $250 million.

At what many would consider retirement age, Harland Sanders started from scratch and built a successful global business that continues to thrive over seventy-five years later.

Success through Service

In my first book, *Is This Seat Taken? Random Encounters That Change Your Life*, I explore the concept that incidental encounters are not incidental at all. In fact, the individuals who cross our paths do so for specific reasons, for one or both of you. Harland Sanders's life, like so many represented in this book, is testimony to this belief. There were two serendipitous meetings, in particular, that were transformational to his life.

The first meeting transpired as a friendly pickup, when he was hitchhiking in Kentucky, which ultimately led to his first job running a service station for Standard Oil. The second meeting was with Pete Harman, who gave him the visibility and backing he needed to launch his initial fried chicken business. Neither of these encounters were planned, strategized, or premeditated. Harland was open to unforeseen opportunities and seized them when they appeared. Due to Harland making the most of both introductions, they resulted in life-transforming opportunities.

As a member of Rotary International, I have a profound respect for the Rotary values that Harland embraced as his guiding compass for his life and his pursuit of being in service. He ensured that every aspect of his business passed the litmus tests of "Is it the truth? Is it fair to all concerned? Will it build goodwill and better friendships? Will it be beneficial to all concerned?" I believe this purity of intention was seminal to his ultimate success. The universal laws of karma dictate that for every action there is an equal and opposite reaction: as we sow, so shall we reap. It is not to say that Harland did not have his challenges and hurdles; he most certainly did. He even went bankrupt several times in his life. However, whatever you put out into the universe will undoubtedly be returned to you, and I believe his intentions of practicing the Rotary motto of "putting service above self" ultimately served him well.

To me, the most inspiring lesson of his life was his unwavering resiliency. None of us will come through life unscathed. All of us will have challenges with varying degrees of severity. Harland Sanders was no exception. He experienced divorce, the death of a child, and financial ruin twice. And the daily ups and downs of his life and business, which may pale in comparison to his other huge hurdles, are not insignificant. Yet he never lost hope. He never gave up. He never lost the belief in himself and his abilities. He vowed to always do his best, in whatever endeavor he undertook. Most importantly, he never lost faith that all would work out if he created the best product he could and continue to provide excellent customer service to his clients.

It is never too late in life to pursue and achieve your dreams. It all comes down to how badly you want to do so. Harland Sanders's tenacity built a life and legacy, representing an "Original Recipe" of success.

Alignment Lessons: Make It Real

- Persistence pays off. Never, never, never give up.

- Seemingly incidental and serendipitous encounters can open doors never expected and completely change your life.

- Service above self trumps everything else.

- Live your life by the Rotary Four Way Test: Is it the truth? Is it fair to all concerned? Will it build goodwill and better friendships? Will it be beneficial for all concerned?

- Have faith that it will all work out exactly as it is supposed to in the end.

Wealth, like happiness, is never attained when sought after directly. It comes as a by-product of providing a useful service.
—**Harland Sanders**

Barbara Miller
West Texas Live Wire

The secret is to take good people who
know what to do and let them work.
—Barbara Miller

When people leave a company job, they are either pushed or they jump. Neither option is for the faint-hearted; they each come with unique challenges. However, when one is pushed at the age of sixty, it has to be daunting. Thus unfolds the story of Barbara Miller.

Barbara's late-in-life story begins in Amarillo, Texas. Amarillo sits in the Texas panhandle, the home of vast, rolling ranches, aromatic acres of wildflowers, and rusty red rock canyons. Those who call Amarillo home resemble the land. They represent the juxtaposition of generous goodwill surrounded by sinewy substance and tough temperaments. Most West

Texans are unselfishly benevolent in nature yet unwavering in their values, their character, and their courage. A West Texan is the singular person you would want in your foxhole. Though Barbara Miller originally hailed from Kansas, she was the epitome of a West Texan.

Barbara was born in 1933 in the tiny town of Elkhart, Kansas, which is located at the far southwestern corner of Kansas butting up against Colorado and Oklahoma. She was reared in her parents' humble two-room farmhouse. I imagine it was here that Barbara and her brother's values were shaped by the example of their hard-working parents. She aspired to attend college, and ultimately moved to Wichita Falls, Texas, to attend Draughon's Business College while also holding down a job in the freight industry to help fund her tuition. At the age of seventeen, Barbara met Lloyd Miller, fell in love, and in 1950 they married and moved to Amarillo.

Lloyd and Barbara began their life together like so many Americans. They moved into a lovely home, began a family, and became involved in the community. They had two children, Patricia and Steven. Not many years later, Barbara went to work for Roberts Paper Company. She loved her work and the industry as well as her fellow employees. Over the next thirty years, she became proficient in her business skills, learned the industry, and enjoyed serving her customers. However, in 1995, an unexpected twist of fate forced her to move out of her comfort zone.

Due to an unforeseen business situation, the company was forced to downsize, and she, along with several of her colleagues, was shown the door. Barbara had been a loyal servant at the company for three decades; now she found herself unemployed. Not certain what to do, she and her colleagues deliberated starting their own paper distribution company. Barbara was a widow, a grandmother of four, and was sixty years old. Despite these stark realities, she joined her colleagues in opening a paper distribution company.

Barbara and her scrappy team of fifteen cobbled together $300,000 in seed capital and opened the company's doors in January 1995. They were tenacious, they were hungry, and they were fearless. Barbara knew there was limited growth of new industrial business in the immediate Amarillo trade area; thus, they needed to gain customers through providing quality products coupled with outstanding service. By building upon these two pillars, the Miller Paper Company attracted clients who had been fulfilling their paper needs through other distributors. Barbara encouraged and incentivized her team to treat their customers the way they would want to be treated. She once said: "Make your customer feel important—because they are! If you lose them, you are out of business." This simple motto served Miller Paper Company well. In their first year, with the initial capitalization of only $300,000, they generated more than $3 million in sales.

However, in these first few years, Barbara's hurdles were not limited solely to her business. Only five months after she opened her doors, she was given a grim prognosis: she was diagnosed with ovarian cancer. When she would normally be worrying about inventory levels, top-line revenue, and assembling a strong leadership team, Barbara was facing the fight for her life. Fortunately, the physicians found the disease in its early stages; however, she still had to endure months of chemotherapy and, subsequently, a bone marrow transplant. Regardless of these monumental hardships, Barbara's West Texas tenacity kicked into full throttle. She empowered her team and demonstrated the solidarity of a committed leader. Later, she would attest that the reason the company continued to grow and thrive during this period was due to the collection of exemplary employees who "knew what they were doing." Her humility is inspiring, and by relinquishing control to her trusted team, there is no question that they had renewed vim and vigor to continue as strong stewards of their enterprise.

Four short years later, Miller Paper Company had grown to a $7 million company, experiencing an average growth rate of 20 percent annually. They were occupying a 50,000-square-foot warehouse with thirty-three employees and providing thousands of products, ranging from towels and toilet paper to upscale wrapping paper and industrial packing material. Barbara had realized that in order for her company to grow she needed to continue with the high-quality products and service strategy, yet she also needed to continue to introduce new products and find new customers. To her, it was as simple as that.

Her aggressive team of fifteen salespeople pursued businesses ranging from prisons and commercial manufacturers to beauty parlors and convenience stores. From her perspective, everyone needed basic paper goods. She was constantly encouraging growth, either with new logos, expansion of customers' existing footprints, or introduction of brand-new offerings to the market.

Over the next few years, Miller Paper began servicing businesses far beyond the Amarillo area, spanning an area of more than 150 square miles and reaching into Oklahoma and New Mexico. Not one to be slow to the dance, Barbara also embraced the Internet and launched the company's e-commerce site early in the Internet boon. For a company founded five short years earlier, these feats astounded even the most cynical naysayers.

Barbara began to be recognized for her entrepreneurial prowess. In 1997, Dun & Bradstreet recognized her company as the sixty-fifth fastest-growing small business in the nation. In 2000, she was named Texas Small Business Person of the Year. She was one of fifty-three budding entrepreneurs to travel to Washington, DC, to receive their award from the Small Business Administration at the White House. The criteria for this award included the growth of the company, overcoming adversity, sustainability, and ongoing support of their community both financially and through their volunteer commitments. The Harvard Business School of New York chose Barbara Miller and her company as one of ten finalists in the America's Entrepreneur Award, 2001.

Despite Barbara's and her team's many business accomplishments, she remained steadfast in her commitment to give back to her community. Though she gave freely of her finances, Barbara was also overwhelmingly generous with her time. She was active in the Amarillo Chamber of Commerce, the Amarillo Women's Network, the United Way, and in the fine arts, serving on the board of the Amarillo Opera and the Beethoven Society of the Amarillo Symphony. In 1998, for her ongoing dedication to vocational excellence and her devotion to serving her community, she received the coveted Sam Walton Leadership Award.

Barbara Miller was most devout in her service to the Rotary Club of Amarillo. She served this organization with perfect attendance throughout her membership. There is no question that she embraced and epitomized the Rotary Four Way Test in her work and life: "Is it the truth? Is it fair to all concerned? Will it build goodwill and better friendships? Will it be beneficial to all concerned?"

In 2005, less than a decade after she founded the fledgling, gutsy company, Barbara Miller succumbed to her battle with cancer at the age of seventy-one. In this relatively short period of time, Barbara had built a multimillion-dollar business from scratch, which served thousands of clients throughout the nation. Her well-founded entrepreneurial vision inspired her team to take the lead, even when she couldn't during her illness. In 2006, the well-respected El Paso firm Gage Van Horn & Associates acquired Miller Paper & Packaging products to extend their offerings.

Barbara Miller established a legacy spanning far beyond her beloved husband, children, grandchildren, and comfortable lifestyle. She did so after the age of sixty due to an unforeseen layoff from a job she'd had for more than thirty years.

When Life Requires Scrappy Resolve

I find that the thousands of baby boomers reinventing their lives post-retirement age fall into three primary categories. First, there are those who have financially "made it," whatever "it" means to that particular person, and they are off to build schools in Nepal, teach history, or start a nonprofit to fulfill their innermost longing to give back to the cause most precious to their heart. Some of the financially free choose the simple "good life" of global travel, golf, and grandchildren. Second, there are those who have the courage to jump off the high board to pursue what they *really* want to do regardless of the consequences. Finally, there are those who by no choice of their own find themselves corporate refugees being laid off unexpectedly without a safety net. This was the case of many of the stories included in this book, including that of Barbara Miller.

Being laid off at age sixty and feeling you don't have "enough" to support you throughout the remainder of your life can be terrifying. Age discrimination is undeniably a factor for employment after a certain age. Uncertainties of a person's relevance in today's business climate can shake self-confidence even in those with the most moxie. Our fears can either paralyze us or serve as our greatest catalyst to take charge of our lives. In Barbara's case, they were catalytic. Rather than choose to take her toys and go home, she challenged her fellow workers to collaborate and create a new company. Traditional convention could have dictated another alternative, but Barbara's

West Texas backbone would have none of it. Her bold, courageous move inspired others to follow; and her passion, commitment, and positive energy attracted more positive can-do spirit. Barbara's story is an example of leadership at its core. It shows pure, raw chutzpah.

And as if being a neophyte bootstrapped entrepreneur weren't enough of a challenge, Barbara was diagnosed with ovarian cancer only five months into the endeavor. At this point, she could have thrown in the towel and probably no one would have questioned her decision. But Barbara's grit was just surfacing. Through multiple rounds of chemotherapy, a bone marrow transplant, and the ongoing daily fight against one of the most formidable cancers, she persevered. As she was once described by a doctor to her son, "She is one tough old bird." Like the familiar phrase, *when the going gets tough, the tough get going,* Barbara Miller took control of her life.

I would like to have known Barbara Miller. I imagine she spoke with a West Texas drawl and that she had a no-nonsense attitude. I doubt she had time for pretense or drama; and I bet she preferred straight talk and firm handshakes. I figure she was enviously revered by men and beloved by women, and that the generosity with which she gave is still being revealed. She shied away from public accolades unless it was to promote her town, her company, or her people. The likes of Barbara Miller are rare and becoming rarer as time goes by. She was an ordinary person thrown into relatively extraordinary conditions. From that Amarillo dust bowl, she molded a vessel that held her life's example as one to appreciate.

Alignment Lessons: Make It Real

- Treat others as you would want to be treated—in business and in life.

- Teamwork in life and in business is everything.

- Keep integrity at the forefront of every decision and every interaction.

- Give quietly. Lead humbly. Give credit where credit is due.

- Put your customers' needs first and serve their needs. The rest will take care of itself.

- If you want to own a company, get on with it.

Every time I wake up, I am just excited to see what the day is going to bring and what the Lord has planned for me.
—Barbara Miller

Ray Kroc
Overnight Success

*If you work just for money, you'll never
make it, but if you love what you're
doing and you always put the customer
first, success will be yours.*
—Ray Kroc

Is there anyone in the world who has not heard of McDonald's? The golden arches are arguably one the most iconic logos in history. The man behind this international brand, Ray Kroc, had a life story that may seem eerily familiar to many people today who are over fifty. Like many of us, Ray had a very normal middle-class upbringing. His father, an immigrant from the Czech Republic, worked at Western Union, and his mother taught piano lessons for extra money while rearing Ray and his younger brother and sister. Ray's mother was fastidious in her quest for cleanliness and often scrubbed the kitchen floor, on her hands and knees, several times a week. Ray loved to help his mother with the housework, and he took particular delight in sweeping. He sought approval, was very eager to please, and wanted things to be as perfect as possible.

Early in his childhood, when Ray was just four years old, his parents were curious about his future, as he had shown pluck even at this early age. They took him to a phrenologist who read the contours of his skull. Phrenology had been widely popular in the late nineteenth century but, by the time the Kroc's had their son "read," the practice had fallen out of fashion. These specialists followed a process that involved observing and feeling the bumps on the skull to determine an individual's psychological attributes. Interestingly, the phrenologist predicted that Ray's future would be in the food service industry.

That future did not wait long to be revealed. The young, enterprising Ray, when still in grade school, opened a lemonade stand on the street in front of his house. The line was long, and his entrepreneurial interest was spiked. This was the first of many food-related jobs Ray held as a young boy. He also worked behind a soda fountain in his uncle's drug store and in a grocery store, informing his view that life was one great big opportunity to sell food to hungry consumers. He held himself to a higher standard than most young people his age, and never took no for an answer. He thrived on making the sale and was relentless in this pursuit.

When Ray was a sophomore in high school, his determined will was given a ripe opportunity. The United States was embroiled in World War I, and Ray wanted to serve. Though he was too young to join the army, he convinced his parents, at the mere age of fifteen, to let him join the Red Cross as an ambulance driver. The war ended before his training finished, and he was never able to serve in this capacity. At this point, uncertain as to what he truly wanted to do, Ray took a job at the Paw Paw Lake resort area in Michigan. It was here that Ray met and began to date Ethel Fleming. After three long years, he finally decided it was time to get married. However, due to the ages of both Ray and Ethel, his father would not give him permission until Ray was steadily employed. Determined to marry Ethel, Ray secured his first job—selling paper cups!

He was a natural. He was a talker and the consummate salesperson. He knew how to work hard, and he was not afraid of long hours. Ray was known for being very buttoned-up and for his spit and polish. Brylcreem, starched shirts, and tightly knotted ties were his standard fare. He was squeaky clean, and his customers loved him.

Not too long after entering the fascinating world of selling paper cups, he stumbled onto a set of clients that would set him on his way back to his old friend, the drugstore soda fountain.

In the 1930s, soda fountains were the mainstay in small-town America. These small diners offered folks an easy in–easy out snack or drink; and every small town or city in the country had at least one soda fountain cafe. Ray was able to convince these owners that they could sell their drinks "to go" using his paper cups. They could get folks in and out faster, ultimately sell more drinks, and increase profits. It was sheer genius! When Ray secured a contract with Walgreens, the largest drugstore chain in the Midwest, he became the star of his company. This was the first entrée into what we now know as the fast-food market.

Ray spent as much time as he could with his customers, often at the expense of his family, learning all he could about what worked well and what didn't work well in their business. His desire to discover ways he could help his clients built his reputation and credibility.

In this ongoing quest, Ray learned about a new device on the market called a Multi-Mixer, which could make five milkshakes at a time instead of just one. He immediately understood that the Multi-Mixer would improve his clients' sales. In 1939, at age thirty-seven, after sixteen years of selling paper cups, Ray left to become the Multi-Mixer's sole distributor.

This calculated risk paid off. In the early 1950s, Ray was making about $25,000 a year, which was a lot of money in those days. However, the business and economic picture in America began to change. The sprawl into the suburbs put pressure on businesses in small towns, and many neighborhood soda fountains were forced to close. As Ray was approaching his fiftieth birthday, he was losing customers by the dozens and feeling a real pinch in his business. In 1954 he met two individuals who would change his life.

One of Ray's clients kept placing large orders for the milk-shake machines, though other soda fountains were closing. He felt compelled to meet these business owners in person and learn what they were doing differently from other businesses, so he caught a plane and flew to San Bernardino, California. Upon arrival, he discovered a small yet successful restaurant owned and run by two brothers, Dick and Mac McDonald.

Back in the 1920s, Dick and Mac had moved to California from New Hampshire. In 1937, after a few odd stints in other vocations, they opened McDonald's, a drive-in eatery they modeled after a successful drive-in hotdog stand in the area. Their customers loved getting the full-menu service without having to leave their automobiles. Dick and Mac grew this into one of the most successful drive-ins in the area. They ran the business successfully for more than eight years. However, after World War II ended, they saw their business begin to change. Americans wanted the "good life" in every aspect of their world— they wanted *what* they wanted *when* and *how* they wanted it. Speed was the catalyst for change. The McDonalds elected to close their successful drive-in and set out to completely reinvent their model. They created an assembly-line approach in the kitchen, incorporating efficiency comparable to a Henry Ford assembly line. They cut their menu from twenty-five items to nine. By focusing on just a few items—burgers, fries, and beverages—they could concentrate on quality at every step.

Ray was struck by the effectiveness of their operation. Not afraid of failure and once again displaying his determined will, Ray grasped the franchising potential of McDonald's, and offered to work as a franchising agent for a cut of the profits. In 1955, at age fifty-three, Ray left his traveling sales career with which he had enjoyed modest success and provided for his family over the past few decades. He made the bold decision to leave his comfort zone and join the McDonald brothers in building out their small restaurant chain. He opened his first McDonald's restaurant that year.

Ray was fanatical about every aspect of his restaurant

being pristine. On the weekends, he could be found sweeping and even scraping gum from the sidewalk in front of this first establishment. This McDonald's had to be perfect, in his estimation, as this was the model on which he would sell the franchise to the rest of the country. Again, his work ethic, attention to detail, and quest for perfection was pervasive in every aspect of his approach to business.

In the first year, he sold eighteen franchises. He was not making much money, however, as his deal with the McDonald brothers was not lucrative for anyone but the brothers. The big shift happened when he met his partner, Harry Sonneborn, who helped Ray create a financial model leveraged on the real estate on which the restaurants would be built. Ray would purchase or lease the land on which all franchises would be located. Franchisees would then have to pay Ray a set monthly rental amount of money for this land, or a percentage of their sales, whichever was greater. This aligned Ray's interest with his franchisees' interest. This win-win philosophy was a key to his ongoing success, and a principle that he would integrate into every aspect of his business going forward.

Ray's goal was to open a thousand franchises from coast to coast, and he traveled relentlessly to accomplish it. His approach to finding these locations was quite unconventional, yet intuitive. He would scout new locations by flying over communities and looking for church steeples, as he believed good American families lived near churches, and those families were his target market. He followed his gut, not fancy quantitative analyses or studies. His approach paid off in spades. From 1958 to 1961, Ray opened more than two hundred franchises.

Ray ran each franchise with a high degree of control; nothing was left to chance or variation by the independent operators. From the width of hamburgers and the number of ounces of ketchup on each sandwich to the standards of cleanliness inside and outside the restaurant, all was outlined with an amazing degree of specificity. His vision was to build a global restaurant system that would be famous for food of consistently high quality and uniform, formulaic methods of preparation. He wanted to serve burgers, buns, fries, and beverages that tasted just the same in Alaska as they did in Alabama. He kept the assembly line approach to hamburger preparation that the McDonald brothers had pioneered and added additional automation, standardization, and discipline. He carefully recruited franchise owners for their ambition and drive, and, raising the level of scrutiny of food preparation to a new height, he put them through an intense indoctrination at the Hamburger University. At the University, franchisees earned certificates in "hamburgerology" with a minor in French fries. Ray Kroc wanted it done his way; his rigor in standardization was legendary. He continued to focus his efforts on growing suburban areas and capturing new markets with familiar food and low prices.

During this period, Ray's unquenchable ambitions began to eclipse those of the McDonald brothers, who squelched many of his ideas. Ray wanted more control over various aspects of the business, so, just six years after embarking on this new and relatively unfamiliar business, when he was fifty-nine years old, Ray bought out the brothers, including their name, for $2.7 million in cash, which put him into tremendous debt. This was an enormous sum of money, and Ray felt that price was similar to extortion, since he felt he had done most of the work. The McDonald brothers had given him the initial idea, but that was basically the extent of their contribution from his perspective. Regardless, he wanted creative control, and it was a price worth paying. Buying out the brothers was his opportunity to unleash his potential, though the outcome was far from certain.

Ray Kroc, then a middle-aged salesperson relatively comfortable in his field, branched out to embark upon large-scale entrepreneurship. He chose a unique path and leveraged his strengths to accomplish his goals. He used his well-honed selling skills to persuade franchisees and suppliers to buy into his vision, working not just *for* McDonald's, but also for themselves, "together with" McDonald's.

He coined the slogan, "In business for yourself, but not *by* yourself." His original philosophy was based on the simple principle of a three-legged stool: one leg was McDonald's; the second, the franchisees; and the third, the McDonald's suppliers. The stool was only as strong as the three legs.

As McDonald's expanded, Ray rewarded creativity in new ideas for new food items. He believed in the entrepreneurial spirit, and rewarded his franchisees for embracing this philosophy as well. Many of McDonald's most famous menu items—like the Big Mac, Filet-O-Fish, and the Egg McMuffin—were created by franchisees. At the same time, the McDonald's values and overall culture insisted franchisees follow the core McDonald's principles of quality, service, cleanliness, and value. Ray had an unwavering passion for quality, which meant that every single ingredient was tested and tasted to meet his standards.

As restaurants boomed, the massive volume of orders

caught the attention of suppliers, who began taking McDonald's standards as seriously as McDonald's did. As other quick-service restaurants began to follow, McDonald's high standards rippled through the meat, produce, and dairy industries. Again, embracing his ongoing belief and philosophy in the power of partnership, Ray wanted to build a collaborative and expansive partnering community with McDonald's suppliers, and he managed to create the most integrated, efficient, and innovative supply system in the food service industry. These supplier relationships have flourished over the decades; in fact, many McDonald's suppliers operating today first started business with a handshake from Ray Kroc.

Right up until he died in 1984 at age eighty-one, Ray Kroc never stopped working for McDonald's. Even when he was confined to a wheelchair, he still went to work in the office in San Diego nearly every day. He would keep an eagle eye over the McDonald's restaurant near his office, phoning the manager to remind him to pick up the trash, clean his lot, and turn on the lights at night.

From his passion for innovation and efficiency to his relentless pursuit of quality and his many charitable contributions, Ray Kroc's legacy continues to be an inspirational, integral part of McDonald's. At the time of his death, McDonald's had 7,500 locations in thirty-one countries and was worth $8 billion. Ray's personal fortune was estimated at $500 million.

Ray Kroc created all this after age fifty-three,
and in the last twenty-eight years of his life.

The Price of Misalignment

In business school we studied McDonald's as the benchmark for entrepreneurship, scalable business models, the power of the brand, and ongoing innovation. Students at the naive age of twenty imagined Ray Kroc, the founder of McDonald's, as an old man—fifty-three was a lifetime away. Numerous after-class discussions centered around our dreams, what businesses we could build, the fortunes we could accumulate, and, in some cases, the books we could write. That future is now. Many of us may believe our time has passed. Our dreams are now either obsolete or unachievable. Ray Kroc's life tells a different story. To a worn-out, middle-class traveling salesman, whose business was suffering a downturn, his life literally turned on a dime.

Once again, a serendipitous encounter introduced someone to a billion-dollar opportunity. Ray took it upon himself to get to know his clients in the spirit of gold-star service, and in the case of the McDonald brothers, opened the door to a fortuitous opportunity. Many of us may have been introduced to individuals who could change our lives and usher in unforeseen profitable pursuits. Ray's distinct differentiator was his fearlessness in pushing himself into a realm with which he was totally unfamiliar. His choice was not impulsive folly; it was bold courageousness to trust his gut instincts. It takes a strong combination of gumption and moxie to leave a relatively predictable career in midlife to enter a field in which you have limited knowledge and virtually no experience. Yet, Ray dove into the fast waters of fast-food franchises with little more than an inner tube for support. He kicked hard and swam even faster to stay afloat.

Ray knew where he was strong, and he also acknowledged where he was not. He was not bashful about admitting his shortcomings, and he made it a standard practice to hire individuals to fill the gaps of his weaknesses. He was ruthless in his pursuit of talent, and he was not intimidated by hiring those who were smarter than he was. He realized that surrounding himself with astute leaders who could pioneer and set the pace for innovation was critical. Fostering a team of diverse talent was a key pillar in his success. He extended his view of teamwork and partnership beyond the four walls of McDonald's, and reached deep into the ecosystem of his suppliers, customers, and extended community. He did this without the benefit of online communities, social media, or even interactive email. He built these relationships the old-fashioned way: through listening and learning what they needed and wanted, and working hard to build a mutually beneficial service and product offering to provide it. These are basic tenets in building a sustainable business, yet they are so often forgotten. As opposed to trying to develop, price, and sell a product the way he wanted to sell it, he aligned his offerings to what his prospective buyers and partners needed and wanted. The rest, as they say, was magic.

Ray made no assumptions that the details would take care of themselves. His zealousness regarding minutiae would make even the most OCD patient cringe. He was adamant about cleanliness, quality, and the rigor surrounding every aspect of his business, building a level of predictability in his work and establishing a standard of reliability for the McDonald's brand. He and the company he was building were consistent in their deliverables: food, quality, ongoing innovation, and shareholder returns. He knew that a person's or company's reputation is their calling card. He held this asset above everything, because he knew that once a person's or company's brand has soured, it is very difficult to change the trajectory.

Relative to Ray Kroc's life, a final observation is that he was professionally aligned. He loved what he did and was exceptional at doing it. And, most importantly, he tied his work to something greater than himself. He wanted to give others the opportunity to work for themselves with a bevy of support from the McDonald's corporate family. He thrived on boosting others to levels of greatness even they could not fathom. There are millions of individuals around the world who have benefitted from Ray's genius, from hourly dishwashers and short-order cooks who flip burgers to entrepreneurial franchise operators who have built generational wealth for their families. Ray Kroc's professional legacy is undeniable and one of great significance.

However, Ray's personal life suffered. By his own admission, he put his work first. Two of his marriages ended in divorce, and he battled a highly destructive relationship with alcohol most of his life. In an upscale piano bar, when he was still married to his second wife, Ray met a stunning blonde piano player named Joan Mansfield. After an ongoing affair, they married twelve years later. Joan was a devoted wife for fifteen years, until Ray's death in 1984. In the end, Ray Kroc seemed to have had it all: fame, fortune, fulfillment, and a loving relationship. It did not all come at one time, nor did it come without pain, hardship, loss, and compromise. Whether we agree with his choices, his style, or his priorities, he lived his life his way and undoubtedly left his mark on the world.

Alignment Lessons: Make It Real

- Always play to your strengths, and surround yourself with those who augment, extend, and complement what you bring to the table.

- Love what you do, be good at it, and tie it to something greater than yourself. Others' success is your success.

- Sweat the small stuff. Pay attention to detail.

- Push yourself out of your comfort zone. Take calculated risks to grow.

- Listen to your gut and follow your intuition.

I was an overnight success all right,
but thirty years is a long, long night.
—Ray Kroc

Bill Wilson
From Addiction to Admirable Legacy

To the world you may be one person,
but to one person you may be the world.
—**Bill Wilson**

Bill Wilson's climb from destitution to altruistic service is legendary. However, at middle age, Bill's life was certainly not one of a model citizen, and how he arrived at this point was equally sad and disturbing.

Bill was born in 1895, at his parents' home in rural Vermont. They owned the Mount Aeolus Inn and Tavern, which catered to business travelers for food, drink, and board. Sadly, early in his childhood, Bill's mother and father unconscionably abandoned him; his father never returned from a purported business trip, and his mother left to study medicine. Bill's maternal grandparents took him and his sister into their home, and embraced them as their own.

Despite this inconceivable disregard by his parents, as a young boy and teenager Bill showed tremendous resolve, determination, and a diversity of talents. He became the captain of his high school football team and the principal violinist of the school orchestra. He was attempting to make the most of his life.

However, Bill began to suffer from serious bouts of depression. His first experience was at the young age of seventeen. His first love, Bertha Bamford, died unexpectedly from complications of surgery, and her death threw him into grief and depression. Depression became a familiar visitor in Bill's life and never completely left.

During the summer of 1913, while sailing on Vermont's Emerald Lake, Bill met Lois Burnham, four years his senior. There was an immediate connection, and two years later they were engaged. Bill enrolled in Norwich University, but depression and ongoing panic attacks forced him to leave after only one semester. The next year he reenrolled and renewed his commitment to his studies. Unfortunately, there was a highly visible hazing incident at the university. No one group of individuals would take responsibility or identify the perpetrators; thus, the entire class was punished. Bill was ultimately suspended for his involvement. His life continued to be riddled with challenges and setbacks, most beyond his control.

In 1916, Bill was drafted to serve in the Vermont National Guard, due to Pancho Villa's incursion into the United States. The following year, Bill was commissioned as an artillery officer.

During his military training in Massachusetts, he took his first drink of alcohol, a glass of beer. He *claimed* that this initial drink had little effect on him. A few weeks later at another dinner party, he drank more potent cocktails, and he immediately began to feel at ease with the guests and liberated from his awkward shyness. As Susan Cheever recounts in her book, *My Name Is Bill,* Bill thought, "I had found the elixir of life. Even that first evening, I got thoroughly drunk, and the next few times I drank, I passed out completely. But as everyone drank hard, not too much was made of that." Bill was in denial. This was the beginning of a dangerous, life-changing cycle in Bill's life. Alcohol became his blanket of comfort, his release from reality, and his escape into an imaginary world that existed only in his muddled mind.

Bill and Lois were married in 1918, right before Bill was drafted as a second lieutenant in the Coast Artillery to serve in World War I. After his military service, he returned to live with Lois in New York. Bill's love affair with alcohol continued, playing havoc in every crevice of his life. He failed to graduate from law school, and his life continued in a downward spiral. Though he became a stock speculator and had some success evaluating companies for potential investors, his constant drinking made business impossible. Lois actually traveled with Bill, hoping to help keep him from his binges; however, this proved difficult, and Bill's drunkenness continued and ultimately ruined his reputation.

In 1933, when Bill was only thirty-eight years old, he was committed to the hospital multiple times under the care of Dr. William Silkworth, whose revolutionary theory was that alcoholism was a matter of both physical and mental control. Discussing his problem with Dr. Silkworth gave Bill hope that alcoholism was indeed a medical condition rather than a moral failing. However, even that knowledge could not help him. He was eventually told that he would either die from his alcoholism or have to be locked up permanently.

Bill was at his lowest point, and his life was spinning recklessly out of control amidst bars, blurs, and binges. Then, in November 1934, his old drinking buddy Ebby Thatcher paid him a visit. Bill was amazed to learn that Ebby had been sober for several weeks under the guidance of the Oxford Group, an evangelical Christian organization. He was interested in getting sober, yet shortly after Ebby visited, Bill was admitted to the hospital for his fourth and final stay, the result of another drinking binge. It was here that Bill experienced what he described as a "spiritual sensation consisting of a bright light, a feeling of ecstasy, and a new serenity." From this point forward, miraculously, Bill never drank again for the remainder of his life.

After this transformation, Bill wanted to help other alcoholics. He joined the evangelical movement, but he was only successful in keeping himself sober. He was constantly tempted to drink again, as his business efforts continued to meet with difficulty and challenge. Then he had the epiphany that in order for him to remain sober, he needed the support and authentic conversations that only other alcoholics could provide.

He began calling numbers in a church directory in search of a support system. He eventually met Dr. Bob Smith, an alcoholic and a member of the evangelical Christian group. In their initial conversation, Bill shared Dr. Silkworth's theory that alcoholism was a physical and mental addiction, not a moral failing. He also shared his belief that the only way he would be able to stay sober was through having an ongoing spiritual experience. This random encounter between Bill and "Dr. Bob" launched a friendship that changed both men's lives.

After hearing Bill's personal experiences, Bob began to pursue the spiritual remedy for his malady with a willingness that he had never before been able to muster. After only a brief relapse, he became sober, and never had another drink of alcohol.

Bill Wilson and Dr. Bob Smith joined hands and began to work with other alcoholics, using their philosophy and spiritual grounding as their foundation. Bill returned to New York, where he began having success helping alcoholics in what he and Bob called "a nameless squad of drunks." In 1938, after about a hundred alcoholics had become sober through their efforts, they decided to promote their program of recovery through the publication of a book, for which Bill was chosen as the primary author. The book, *Alcoholics Anonymous*, included the list of their suggested activities for spiritual growth, which ultimately became known as the Twelve Steps. Their movement took on the name of their book.

Bill's life hit a crossroads midway and changed course, ultimately leading to a life of tremendous contribution. Alcoholics Anonymous (AA) has provided international fellowship for more than two million members, who belong to more than a hundred thousand groups of alcoholics, which help other alcoholics achieve and maintain sobriety. Admirably, following AA's tradition of sacred anonymity, Bill Wilson was always commonly known as "Bill W." or "Bill." It was only after his death in 1971, at the age of seventy-six, when his name was published in his obituary, that he became known by his full name.

Bill Wilson is perhaps best known as a synthesizer of ideas, the man who pulled together various threads of psychology, theology, and democracy into a workable and life-saving system. Aldous Huxley referred to him as "the greatest social architect of our century," and *Time* magazine included him on its list of the most important people of the twentieth century. Bill modestly described himself as a man who, "because of his bitter experience, discovered, slowly and through a conversion experience, a system of behavior and a series of actions that work for alcoholics who want to stop drinking." Finally, as biographer Susan Cheever wrote in *My Name Is Bill*, "Bill Wilson never held himself up as a model: he only hoped to help other people by sharing his own experience, strength, and hope. He insisted again and again that he was just an ordinary man."

Bill Wilson completely transformed his life, changed the face of alcoholism, and impacted the lives of millions—all after the age of forty-three.

Taking the First Step

The wisdom of the Twelve Steps included in Bill W.'s book, *Alcoholics Anonymous*, is timeless and continues to transform lives nearly seventy-five years later. They are embraced by people recovering from various forms of substance abuse and those recovering from assorted pathologies. I have witnessed many individuals who were not facing chemical dependencies yet also gained heightened self-awareness, strength of conviction, and a "peace that passes all understanding" through embracing these truisms. Thus, the Twelve Steps are included in the synopsis of Bill W.'s biographical study, as one of the many contributions he made to the world through his life's work:

1. We admitted we were powerless over alcohol—that our lives had become unmanageable.

2. Came to believe that a power greater than ourselves could restore us to sanity.

3. Made a decision to turn our will and our lives over to the care of God *as we understood Him.*

4. Made a searching and fearless moral inventory of ourselves.

5. Admitted to God, to ourselves, and to another human being the exact nature of our wrongs.

6. Were entirely ready to have God remove all these defects of character.

7. Humbly asked Him to remove our shortcomings.

8. Made a list of all persons we had harmed, and became willing to make amends to them all.

9. Made direct amends to such people wherever possible, except when to do so would injure them or others.

10. Continued to take personal inventory, and when we were wrong, promptly admitted it.

11. Sought through prayer and meditation to improve our conscious contact with God *as we understood Him*, praying only for knowledge of His will for us and the power to carry that out.

12. Having had a spiritual awakening as the result of these steps, we tried to carry this message to alcoholics, and to practice these principles in all our affairs.

When an individual is aligned, they become their most powerful versions of themselves. Bill W. ultimately became aligned within himself and with a divine power greater than himself. When I think about the concept of alignment, I believe it happens when someone loves what they do, when they are good at it, and when their work is tied to something greater than themselves. Once an individual is truly aligned around their purpose, they begin to live their life on purpose. Bill W.'s life was not always this way, yet through his challenges he developed a greater sense of congruency and ultimately total alignment. As Rilke so beautifully wrote: "Go into yourself and test the deeps in which your life takes rise." Bill W. did this, and through the deeps he found his calling. He knew himself. He embraced himself—his gifts and talents as well as his shadows. He knew his own true sense of belonging. He listened to his inner voice, and ultimately, his thoughts, feelings, beliefs, gifts, talents, strengths, preferences, and desires regarding how and where to contribute in the world became aligned. He remained in the human condition, and faced his demons as we all do every day. But he aligned himself to something greater than himself, and thus he revealed his most powerful, aligned self.

Finally, again, as with so many individuals throughout this book, an incidental encounter completely transformed Bill's life. From a random phone call made during a dark night of the soul, Bill met Dr. Bob. The meeting began a relationship founded on vulnerability, yet built on the bedrock of mutual and perpetual growth. Through the paradox of human weakness and spiritual strength came an unlikely friendship that ultimately not only changed their lives, but the millions of lives they touched.

Alignment Lessons: Make It Real

- Believe in and align yourself to a power greater than yourself.

- The right answers will come after you relax and let your intuition guide you.

- Take action. "You can't think your way into right action, but you can act your way into right thinking."

- Surround yourself with those you can help and who can help you. We are all in this together, and we are connected and in partnership on this planet.

Let Go and Let God.
—Bill Wilson

Jacqueline Qualls
Writing a New Legacy

*It never even occurred to me that I
couldn't do it. I was reared to believe I
could do anything . . . and that basically
meant anything I set my mind to do.*
—**Jacqueline Qualls**

Jacqueline Qualls is a Southern girl to her core. Reared with her three siblings in a small town in East Tennessee, the rhythm of her early life was slow and steady. There was comfort in the cadence of the Southern drawls, and folks treasured familiar kitchen-table talk above most everything else in the world. Jacquie's parents were working class, and money was often scarce. Yet they longed for little and found pleasure in the simplest things. Jacquie was close to her family, particularly to her dad, whom she credits with having given her many of the core principles that guide her today.

Jacquie's father was a very bright man despite having only gone to school through the third grade. His strong work ethic and ability to build strong relationships opened doors and created many unexpected opportunities. His *joie de vivre* was contagious. Though he tried his hand at various jobs and opened many small businesses, he usually left these ventures for what appeared to be the "sure-thing" paycheck, only to return home due to a plant closing or an unforeseen lay-off. Yet Jacquie's father was not a quitter. He was resilient, resourceful, and had a unique gift for finding ways to make money to support his family. These traits were ingrained in Jacquie, sustaining her throughout her life.

Jacquie was the eldest child and, given their financial situation, college was not an option for her. Her father, like many of that era, encouraged his daughter to get a job working for a large, stable corporation that would provide benefits and enable her to save enough for retirement. He never suggested that she should try to find her passion or follow her dreams. It probably didn't occur to him, since he considered the purpose of work to be the ability to survive. This was what he had lived and learned through his life's experience and what he passed on to his children. Jacquie revered her father; his voice reverberated in her mind as she grew into adulthood.

Soon after graduating, Jacquie married her high school sweetheart and moved to the big city of Nashville. She suddenly found herself in the same situation her father had been when she was a child: unemployed and looking for a job. Fresh out of high school with no college degree or experience, she was faced with a harsh reality. The corporate job with benefits was not as easy to attain as she had once thought. She had unwavering self-confidence, however, and knew that if someone would give her the chance, she would be the best employee they ever had. She recalled one job interview in which she actually begged for the job with a "heartfelt promise that they would never regret their decision." She got the job!

Over the next several years, Jacquie changed jobs many times, seeking greater opportunities, always striving for the top in whatever field she chose. During the late 1960s, it was difficult for women to advance and make substantial money. Women typically were paid less than half what men were paid for doing the same job. Jacquie found herself mirroring her father's experience; she was trapped in her life. Just like her father, her life became about survival. She was rearing two children in a double-income working household. It was not the dream she had envisioned as a little girl.

The economy was tight, and the company for which Jacquie worked was in serious financial trouble. As a child, she had watched her family's funds dwindle due to the instability of her father's job status; and now she was concerned it was just a matter of time before she would be let go. She began to look for other opportunities and was referred to a steel company that was looking for an office manager. On a lunch break one day, she went to their office and filled out an application. As she was leaving, it began to pour, so she grabbed her umbrella and sloshed hastily through the parking lot. It was storming so badly that the wind caught her umbrella, turning it inside out, and it flew out of her hands and into the stormy sky. As she stood there getting drenched by the deluge, a car turned into the parking lot and a gentleman wearing a high-end business suit and tie jumped out, caught the umbrella, and brought it to her.

Flabbergasted and reassured that chivalry was not dead, she thanked him profusely. He asked her if he could be of any further assistance, and then he invited her to lunch. Coincidentally, the man was the sales manager at the steel company where she'd just applied. Back at her office later that afternoon, she received a call from the steel company inviting her for a second interview, this time for a sales job. She was hired. This incidental chance encounter launched what was to evolve into a twenty-five-year career.

Jacquie's career in the steel industry began as an inside sales representative, and she was soon promoted to outside sales. She had no experience in this field and navigated a very steep learning curve through determination and an iron will to succeed. She secured her company's largest automotive account and continued to negotiate multimillion dollar contracts within the automotive industry. She was one of a very few women in the predominantly male industry. She continued to work hard and achieved a sterling reputation and track record in what she thought would be her last career. She had achieved what her father thought was the ultimate job: working for a large corporation with benefits and the hope of a nice retirement. And the bonus: Jacquie loved what she did, and she was good at it. She was at the top of her game. However, her professional story was just beginning to unfold.

In 2008, due to the economic recession and an unexpected corporate merger, Jacquie was devastated to receive a pink slip and a small severance package after almost twenty-five years with the company. She was sixty-two years old. She was disillusioned; she had always thought that if she worked hard and did all the "right" things, she would have a position secured by company loyalty and her esteemed sales record. Yet, due to a set of circumstances totally outside of her control and having nothing to do with her job performance, she found herself unemployed for the first time since she graduated high school. She had been working for forty-five years, but she was not able to fully retire. She had no idea what she was going to do.

Her next turn was to be as sharp as a hairpin curve. When a complete stranger told her about a multilevel marketing opportunity in the direct sales industry, she looked into it even though she knew absolutely nothing about the skin care market, other than her own personal skin care habits. She knew she would be starting over in unfamiliar territory, but she also believed she had nothing to lose. She realized she wanted more control over her life, more flexibility and time freedom, and more control over her paycheck. She wanted to make her own money and be her own boss. This direct sales opportunity offered her all of these things, as well as residual income from the business she would build.

Jacquie had learned through her recent experience that there was little security in the traditional business model. She had given her prior employer a large piece of her life, and when hard decisions were made within the company, she was a casualty. The hard realization was that when her prior company needed to cut costs, it was irrelevant how doing so impacted an individual. Jacquie did not want to ever be in that position again. Thus, she took the plunge and began what would become a life-altering career.

Jacquie learned early that the direct marketing industry required a three- to five-year business model. She realized it would take that long to achieve the level of financial success she needed and wanted. Thus, she made a conscious decision to give her new career a minimum of five years. She realized that in this field a person must choose to persevere or they would perish. Quitting was the only sure way to fail, and she was not a quitter. She'd learned this invaluable trait from her father, and once again, it was the gift from him that kept on giving.

Jacquie's children were grown and had moved away from home, her husband had passed away many years before, and she had a very limited network; because she'd been consumed by her corporate job and life at the steel company, most of her friends were in that industry. If she were to succeed in this new venture, she knew she would have to build new networks and share her message with people she did not know. She pursued this with energy and passion and resumed her old habits of working hard and striving to get to the top. But this time it would be different. She was working for herself, on her own terms, and making her own money.

It was not easy. Rejections were common, and judgmental commentary, especially from her former corporate arena, was frequent and harsh. Yet she persevered. She knew her new company was on sure footing, backed by a multibillion dollar brand, and was led by a team of seasoned and highly successful leaders. Over time, she realized a second passion: educating and mentoring others as she built her nationwide team. It gave her tremendous joy to help others achieve their dreams and build their financial freedom.

Jacquie was also overcoming some of her personal fears. As a child, her family moved frequently as her father sought work. She was often ridiculed in school because of her heavy Southern accent. She was paralyzed by the thought of speaking in front of a room of people. In her new profession, she was often called upon to speak and share her story with hundreds and even thousands of skeptical listeners. She grasped this challenge hungrily and captivated her audiences with her vulnerable authenticity and straight-talking manner. People could relate to her, which made her leadership style contagious.

Jacquie's definition of success was far more than a six-figure paycheck. She was becoming successful by her own definition as she was tackling her fears, building new life-long relationships, and helping others achieve their dreams.

Though Jacquie's father had passed away more than fifteen years before and had not left her an inheritance or provided a formal education for her while he was still alive, he had given her gifts that left indelible imprints on her life. Jacquie says, "He instilled in me a strong work ethic and the confidence that all things are possible, no matter what you desire. To always strive for the top and know the sky is the limit. Success results more from your attitude than your ability. That a love for others can help you achieve great things and it's never too late to start over if you are willing to work hard to achieve results. After all, he had started over many times."

Four years after Jacquie embarked on this new professional journey, she had succeeded by every measure. She took hold of her destiny at an age when many give up and think it's too late to start over and condensed a twenty-five-year career into twenty-four months. She now represents a reputable skin care company, led by a team of notable dermatologists, and has built her own seven-figure independent consultancy. She has obtained financial security for her family by rewriting her own legacy at an age when many believe their life is entering the sunset years. She has tapped into the secret that when you help others, the rewards keep coming. Jacquie is zealous about the importance of a Plan B, and she knows that there are no guarantees in life. She is proof positive that you can be successful no matter what your age, even without experience in a given field. It all starts with a desire to achieve and the belief that if anyone else can do it, then why not you?

At the age of sixty-two, Jacquie, a widow, was laid off and wasn't ready for retirement. She embarked on an entirely new career and quest for financial freedom. In 2013, at the age of sixty-seven, she completed her five-year commitment to her direct selling business and achieved total freedom, which she defines as both financial freedom and freedom with her time.

Making up Your Mind

Hearing Jacquie's sweet, syrupy Southern drawl for the first time over the phone is an elixir to the soul. It is both alluringly comforting and astonishingly compelling. It could be easy to conjure up an image of a pushover in a petticoat; however, this would be a misnomer. Jacquie is the antithesis of a wavering, weak woman. She is the purest definition of a steel magnolia. Like steel, the industry from which she initially hailed, fiery heat only intensifies her resolve.

By some societal standards, at age sixty-two, a person often finds him- or herself meandering down easy street. Not so for Jacquie. She was facing a reality many face today: she did not have "enough" to retire in the manner she desired. She did not have a partner to create a cushion—financial or emotional—from the blows she bore. Solitarily, she owned her reality. The magic was that she *knew* this. She knew she had to take responsibility for what would ultimately ensue. And she did.

We can all learn from this example. We don't control the experiences that happen *to* us, or *for* us (depending on how you wish to view the purpose of our daily travails). Yet we do own our choices, our level of discipline, the depths of our convictions, and our sustained mindset. Unfortunately, we cannot pawn those off on anyone else. Both our positive and challenging experiences teach us life lessons. If we are still on the planet, then we are still enrolled in "Earth school." Thus, if you find yourself at fifty-five and not where you thought you would be, or at sixty-two and unemployed, or at seventy-five with depleted retirement funds, you have an opportunity to change your trajectory and *learn*. And learn you must—then you take charge.

The second lesson I gleaned from Jacquie was her unshakable optimism and belief in herself. She believed that if she worked hard and helped others along the way, she would be successful. She was a neophyte in her new industry and had zero experience in the skin care industry into which she would be selling. But never for one instant did she doubt her ability to do the job and reach her goals. Her fervent unflappable faith was her propellant. Anyone who has ever attempted a career in direct sales knows that the rate of rejection can be demoralizing. Yet Jacquie's mindset was not geared that way. She chose instead to see the potential, seize the opportunity, and resolve never to quit. She believed that each "no" led her to her next "yes." She had dozens of doors shut on her, phone calls not returned, and individuals join her team only to quit shortly thereafter. She knew the business was not for the fainthearted, yet she believed it *was* for the person who could grasp the vision of a multifigure residual income. She clutched that vision with both hands and never looked back.

It is difficult to limit the lessons I learned from my exposure to Jacquie. However, my final insight is that Jacquie's ongoing mantra was to be a part of something greater than herself. In my first book, *Is This Seat Taken? Random Encounters That Change Your Life,* the third prong of how I defined living a fully aligned and fulfilled life is to have your North Star tied to something greater than yourself. This varies for each person. For Jacquie, it is not only about creating a sustainable income for herself, her son, daughter, and grandchildren; it is also about helping others change *their* lives. Her driving motivation is to help as many others as she can to realize the dream she has manifested in her own life. The beauty of this magical mantra is that energy begets energy. As Sarah Bernhardt stated: "Life begets life. Energy creates energy. It is by spending oneself that one becomes rich."

Placing her attention and focusing her energy on helping others, with purity of intention, fills Jacquie's coffers. In her direct sales career, the results speak for themselves.

In each of our lives, we have the same opportunity. The sister lesson to this basic truth of the law of attraction was Jacquie's choice to not resist the hand that she had been dealt at age sixty-two. She made the decision to not resist the fact that she lost her long-standing position. She simply accepted it and moved forward. Again, this was a self-defining moment. As Carl Jung stated so wisely many years ago, "What you resist not only persists, but will grow in size." Had she muddled and fuddled in self-pity, pining for her old position and refusing to accept, embrace, and move on, the situation would have persisted and increased in severity. She recognized she was at a crossroads and looked toward the future with confidence. She steadied herself with a positive mindset, earnestly believing she could create a new life, realize a new dream, and help others achieve the same. And she did just that.

Alignment Lessons: Make It Real

- Think differently. Change that little voice in your head and believe it is never too late to start over. Your mindset is everything.

- Know that it all starts with your belief, no matter what your situation.

- You can achieve greater things than you ever could have imagined if you are willing to work hard, be consistent with your efforts, and know that all things are truly possible.

- Give yourself permission to dream.

- Embrace the gifts from Jacquie's dad: confidence, passion, acceptance, and a strong work ethic, coupled with values and the wisdom to make a difference.

You must take personal responsibility. You cannot change the circumstances, the seasons, or the wind, but you can change yourself. That is something you have charge of.
—Jacqueline Qualls

Photo courtesy of the *Corpus Christi Caller-Times*. Photographer: Bill Olive.

Dorothy Winn
Providential Purpose

I had then, and always will have,
the freedom to choose.
—Dorothy Winn

My first impression of Dorothy Winn brought to mind memories of the fictional character Miss Jane Pittman, made famous by actor Cicely Tyson in the TV film of the same name released in 1974. Her wiry, size-two frame moved with spunk, fortitude, and a centered presence serving as her virtual steel backbone. When I met with her, she had recently relocated to Waxahachie, Texas, to begin yet another chapter in her determined walk through life. As we spoke over lunch, her exuberant sharing of her story was openly vulnerable, yet laced with strength of conviction fueled by a source greater than herself. Her life's journey had been a series of gnarly knots, which taught her the power of choice, resolution, and faith. These lessons are now guideposts as she supports others through their most dire human experiences. No one could have predicted that her life, after navigating numerous hairpin curves and setbacks, would arrive where it has.

In the early 1950s, Dorothy Winn was the first of twelve children born to her sharecropper parents in the small rural town of Lexington, Texas. Dorothy openly admits their family was one of dysfunction and mental illness. She, in fact, had been the product of sexual abuse; yet her mother married her father. It was what was often done in the world into which she was born and reared.

As a family of migrant workers, they seasonally traveled to farming towns to pick cotton and fruits and vegetables, enduring year after year of bitter harvests. They lived a meager life; the average weekly pay for migrant workers at that time was a mere $26, barely enough to provide the necessities of life. Thus, all the children needed to work to put food in their mouths. Dorothy's parents had only gone to school through the third grade. The only life they knew was living day by day and constantly moving from crop to crop, doing hard physical labor in conditions that the majority of American workers would have considered too demeaning, demanding, and low-paying to even contemplate.

Early in life, Dorothy endured unfathomable hardship, abuse, and even death. Two of her youngest siblings died in infancy and her mother, only twelve years older than Dorothy, passed away at a very young age, leaving Dorothy to look after her younger siblings. Seeking some semblance of normalcy, her father moved the family to Baytown, Texas, where he found odd jobs to support his children. Dorothy continued in her role of makeshift mother for her younger brothers and sisters while managing to attain her high school diploma. She was the only one of her family to reach this milestone, and steppingstone to great opportunities later in life.

During these early years, one memory of hope stood out for Dorothy. Faith and spirituality were not grounding forces in their home, but Dorothy's grandmother was a central figure in her life. Dorothy vividly remembers the large Bible her grandmother read daily, recalling the gold-leaf edges and the old indented finger tabs for the various chapters in both the Old and New Testaments. She recalls flipping through it to find the rich, colorful pictures depicting the parables and other historic stories such as David and Goliath, the parting of the Red Sea, and the feeding of the five thousand. These memories were seeds planted early in Dorothy's life. Unbeknownst to her, they would blossom vibrantly late in her life.

As Dorothy openly admits, she was looking for an escape from the mundane claustrophobic life of chief cook and caretaker of her family. So when one of her suitors asked for her hand in marriage, she readily accepted. She and her husband escaped to Corpus Christi to embark on their new life together. Early in their marriage, one of Dorothy's sisters passed away suddenly, leaving her as the unintended adoptive mother of her toddler niece and nephew. She accepted this responsibility with open arms, as she did most occurrences in her life, believing it was providential in nature. Unfortunately, however, the dream of a fairy tale marriage did not materialize. Her husband began to verbally and physically abuse her, and when he also threatened to hurt the children, Dorothy made the decision to leave. She was only twenty-seven years old.

Saddled with two children and with only a high school education, Dorothy had no idea how she was going to make ends meet. She defaulted to a trade she knew only too well: cleaning houses. She embraced this life with betterment for her new family as her guiding force. For more than twenty years, she scrubbed tile floors on her hands and knees, cleaned toilets, and polished silver for a steady roster of clients. Then, one day, what could have been a normal exchange between two women became a life-altering fork in the road for Dorothy.

She had spent the morning buffing and polishing the original hardwood floors at the large palatial estate home of one of her long-term clients. The owner had very high expectations that had been formed through years of drinking the proverbial high-society Kool-Aid of Corpus Christi's wealthy households. As she came into the dining room to inspect Dorothy's work, she commented how the baseboards were not as pristine as she had hoped and wondered why Dorothy had not used a toothbrush on them to achieve the high gloss she desired. It was then that Dorothy had her epiphany. She wondered if using a toothbrush to clean the four-inch baseboards for less than minimum wage was her life's destiny. At that very moment, she made the choice to begin creating the life she wanted for herself and her newly adopted children.

Dorothy had been attending church regularly since moving to Corpus Christi, and she had developed a strong relationship with one of the pastors. She shared with him her idea to start a cleaning service for commercial organizations, and they jointly founded the Emmanuel Cleaning Service. Dorothy's honest, forthright approach won the first business client's support, and their company was born. They built their business into a substantial enterprise, giving Dorothy a newly found self-confidence and a more comfortable financial cushion than she had ever had.

They ran the business profitably for more than seven years. As their business began to scale, her clientele continued to request Dorothy's personal attention, which became increasingly difficult due to sheer lack of time and stamina. In addition, it was difficult to find and employ staff members who would cater to her customers' whims the way she had. Thus, due to their inability to harness the growing pains of their budding business, she and her pastor partner decided to sell their company. Again, she was at a crossroads.

Dorothy and the pastor parted ways, each following their own path. He went back to school, and she made the decision to pursue her teaching degree. She had left school thirty years earlier.

Though Dorothy's path was unclear, she recalls hearing a voice echoing Psalm 46:10: "Be still and know that I am God." Dorothy's belief in her providential plan sustained her. She never wavered in her knowledge that as long as she worked hard, her material needs would be addressed. Unbeknownst to her, while she was attending school and moving in a direction that was not well defined, an anonymous person suggested to a supervisor at a trauma hospital in Corpus Christi that she join the residency program for chaplains. She received a call from the supervisor, interviewed, and was chosen to join the program. She never found out who had referred her, but she realized that the experience was her destiny.

That voice brought her to Waxahachie. Through her ambiguous period, Dorothy said that it was the still, small voice in her heart that led her to pursue what she now considers her calling. Despite having no early exposure to church or other religious affiliations, over her adult years, she realized each of her experiences had a common denominator. The seeds planted by her grandmother, her acceptance and encouragement by her church through her most difficult years, and, ultimately, her business partnership with her pastor were tied together by a faith-centered foundation.

Dorothy made the decision to become a chaplain and began the rigorous path to attain the required degree and certification. Initially, she thought she was a most unlikely candidate, as her only images of chaplains were men in the military, and she was neither. Yet she followed her heart and made the choice to pursue a new career. It was through this process, late in her life, that her ultimate destiny would unfold.

Dorothy cleaned houses to put herself through rigorous schooling at night. After two long years and more than four hundred hours of classroom instruction, practical application, and study, Dorothy was awarded her healthcare chaplaincy certificate. She has served in this capacity and helped countless families through their most difficult challenges. She has been the trusted adviser and counselor for many individuals through terminal illnesses, challenging decisions, and death. Her faith is unwavering and her devotion humble and authentic. At sixty-two, Dorothy has endured many difficult stages in life. There have been days and years when meals or even a roof over her head were not guaranteed. There were periods when abusiveness was the norm and the weight of this reality was almost unbearable. Yet the constants for Dorothy were two realities: she had the free will to choose how she would deal with the situation, and she had a faith that Providence was the buttress giving her the fortitude to keep moving forward.

Dorothy Winn redefined her life and her definition of success, and found contentment after the age of sixty.

Steel Clothed in a Down Comforter

Dorothy Winn's warmth belies her fortitude, which grew stronger the tougher the challenge. Dorothy's hardy fabric was forged by a complex combination of abuse, rape, betrayal, disrespect, choice, and faith. What began as a life of deflating experiences ultimately became the very fulcrum on which her destiny was revealed.

Dorothy's quiet demeanor and reverent attention to every word builds a bridge of trust. Even to a perfect stranger, her confidence encourages revelation of the darkest corners of one's journey. The beginning of Dorothy's life was not safe, secure, or even promising. However, the spirit of trust and generosity with which she now greets the individuals in her life is palpable. Ironically, the genesis of her trust and generosity is the lack of someone or something in her own life to depend on. She fills this void and offers this safe haven to others. From this authentic position, she attracts and fosters the same, creating a never-ceasing source of replenishment.

Dorothy may not be rich by the standards of many, but she never aspired to be. Her life's riches are measured by different metrics. Spreading love, giving hope, and allowing many to cleave to the bosom of her heart, when they had no other source of care, created a life of great significance and impact for many. Virgil's wisdom rings true here: "Love begets love, love knows no rules, and this is the same for all." Love is the great equalizer and unifier. Dorothy's life epitomizes this. She did not always have the clarity of her life's purpose. She wasn't a child prodigy whose destiny was mapped at an early age. She wasn't a dot-com mogul who was financially successful by the age of thirty-five. Dorothy's life is a story of tight knots and broken strings, which provided the tangled backstory to her life's colorful tapestry.

One final characteristic of Dorothy's I noticed was that her overarching spirit of abundance comes from her fervent belief that all her needs will be met. She is not materially wealthy by anyone's standard, yet she is rich beyond measure. Her life is full in ways not measured by square footage, bank accounts, or the model of car she drives. She makes meaning in her world through the lives she touches, the comfort she fosters, and the grace she gives and ultimately gets through her experiences.

Alignment Lessons: Make It Real

- We always have a choice. Always.

- There is such a thing as Providence; paying attention to these occurrences can open doors we did not initially see.

- The adversities experienced early in life prepare us for the contributions we are to ultimately make.

- What does not kill us undeniably makes us stronger.

At the root of it all, we must remember to
"Be still and know that I am God."
—Dorothy Winn

Don Arnold/Getty Images

Li Cunxin
Dancing an Unexpected Life

In order to fly, you have to be free.
—Li Cunxin

When one first learns about Li Cunxin, one would likely think he was born centuries ago, as the extreme circumstances of his early life are hard to imagine today. Cunxin was born into what would appear a sealed fate as an impoverished peasant destined to be poor and forever insignificant on the world's stage. Yet his life has been speckled with fate-altering twists and turns. At the age of fifty-three, his triumphs continue.

Cunxin was born in 1961 during the reign of Chairman Mao in the communist state of the People's Republic of China. During this tumultuous period in China's history, it is well documented that 35–40 million people suffered and died of starvation between 1959 and 1962. Cunxin's family was among those experiencing unthinkable hardship. His mother and father could neither read nor write, and scraped out a meager farming existence for themselves and their seven sons in a rocky hillside village in the Shandong Province. Many a night, the family would look into their mother's desperate eyes as she placed the evening supper on the table, realizing there was not enough to curb their incessant pangs of hunger. Their crude rock hut had neither running water nor heat to warm them when the thermostat fell to twenty degrees below zero, a temperature typical in this region. The government enforced rigid restrictions, allowing only a few short hours of public electricity in the evenings. Cunxin's childhood was far from ideal, and like his father and grandfather, he held little hope for a life outside of this reality.

One day in the one-room, unheated schoolhouse where he attended class, a group of four government dignitaries came to visit. After the teacher instructed the forty students to stand and sing songs praising Chairman Mao to show their allegiance to their country's leader, the commanding officers explained that they were cultural advisers sent to select a few boys and girls to be part of Madame Mao's Beijing Dance Academy. After highly scrutinizing the students, they chose one little girl to join them. As they exited the schoolhouse, Cunxin's teacher hesitantly extended her arm and touched the last officer on the shoulder, and, pointing at Cunxin, said sheepishly, "What about this one?" Amazingly, they chose Cunxin to join the thousands of children who would go through intense testing for the opportunity to join Mao's cultural revolutionary efforts at the Peking Dance Academy. When Cunxin's teacher was asked many years later why she felt compelled to stop the intimidating officer and recommend Cunxin, she recalled that she had no particular reason other than she felt an urge to do so, and she knew that Cunxin could run fast when playing with the other children. This unexpected and unceremonious action by his teacher started an avalanche of life experiences for Cunxin.

The physical examinations and harsh interrogations to qualify to join the academy were grueling. The candidates had to demonstrate specific physical capabilities to be chosen. Cunxin's legs were held taut and raised high above his head to predict flexibility and malleability. In this excruciating process, both his hamstring muscles were torn; yet he never uttered a sound, as he believed this was his one chance at another life. At eleven years of age, Cunxin was admitted into the academy, leaving his humble life with his family in China forever.

For the next seven years at the academy, the heart-wrenching yearning for his family was nearly overwhelming. Desperately homesick, Cunxin cried himself to sleep almost every night. But his conviction was steadfast, as he was determined to become the best dancer he could. While there, he endured sixteen-hour days of grueling training, six days a week.

While recounting his experiences at the academy, Cunxin recalled a favorite fable his father taught him. The fable concerned a frog who lived in a small, deep well. The frog knew nothing about the outside world. His well and the sky he could see above it were his entire universe.

One day he met a frog who lived in the world above his

well. "Why don't you come down and play with me? It's fun down here," the frog in the deep well asked.

"What's down there?" the frog above asked.

"We have everything down here. We have streams, the undercurrent, the stars, and even the occasional moon," the frog in the well answered.

The frog on land sighed. "My friend, you live in a confined world. You haven't seen what's out here in the much bigger world."

The frog below was very annoyed. "Are you telling me that you have a bigger world than ours? I don't think so . . . as my world is big. We see and experience everything your world has to offer," the well frog said.

"No, you are mistaken. You can only see the world above you through the opening of your well. The world is much, much larger. In fact, it is enormous. I wish I could show you just how big it is," the frog above replied.

The frog in the well became angry. "I don't believe you!" He told his father about his conversation with the frog on the land. "My son," his father said with a saddened heart, "your friend is right. I have heard there is a much bigger world up there, with many more stars than we can see from here."

"Why didn't you tell me about it earlier?" the little frog asked.

"What's the use?" his father replied. "Your destiny is down here in the well. There is no way you can escape."

The little frog said, "I can get out of here. Let me show you!" He jumped and hopped, but the well was too deep.

"It is no use, my son. I have tried all my life and so did your forefathers. Forget the world above. Be satisfied with what you have, or it will cause you such misery in life."

"I want to get out," the little frog cried determinedly. "I want to see the big world above!"

"No, my son," his dad replied. "Accept fate. Learn to live with what is given."

So the poor little frog spent his life trying to escape the dark, cold well. But he couldn't. The big world above remained only a dream.

"Dad, are we in a well?" Cunxin asked his father.

His father thought for a while, careful of the message he would convey to his son. He responded: "It depends on how you look at it. If you look at where we are from Heaven, yes, we are in a well. If you look at us from below, we are not in a well."

"Father, would you call where we are Heaven?"

"No, definitely not," his father replied.

From the time Cunxin was a little boy, he believed the circumstances he was born into were his fate. Since he had been given the opportunity to get out of his well, he was determined not to squander it. He had worked tremendously hard for seven years when fate changed his direction again. In 1979, when he was eighteen and still at the academy, Cunxin was awarded one of the first cultural scholarships to go to America with the financial support of the central government of the People's Republic of China. In America, he joined Ben Stevenson's Houston Ballet as an exchange student. Cunxin had never had exposure to so many of the experiences this opportunity afforded. The cultural divide between his small village in the rural mountains of China and the bustling, moneyed metropolis of Houston was colossal. However, Stevenson and his supporters took Cunxin under their wings and nurtured his growth and integration into the ballet company and Houston society.

While there, Cunxin began to fraternize with Elizabeth Mackey, a young American dancer. They gradually fell in love. Their love affair was unsuspected by everyone, until Cunxin, facing an imminent return to communist China, asked Elizabeth to marry him so he could avoid deportation. This particular action spawned an international incident in 1981, culminating in a twenty-one-hour interrogation of Cunxin while he was being held captive in the Consulate General of the People's Republic of China in Houston. The FBI surrounded the consulate while Chinese and American diplomats negotiated the situation. This high-level scrutiny even included the involvement of then Vice President George H.W. Bush. The issue was ultimately resolved and Cunxin was allowed to stay, though he had to give up his Chinese citizenship.

Li's dancing career blossomed. He became one of the most notable dancers in the world, and he won one bronze and two silver medals in international competitions. Though his first marriage ended in divorce, Cunxin found love again with another dancer, Mary McKendry, whom he met while still in Houston. They married, and in 1995, they moved to Australia, Mary's home, with their three children. His final three-and-a-half years as a principal dancer were spent with the Australian Ballet.

Cunxin began to feel concern for his ability to provide for his family once he was no longer able to perform, and he also felt a strong unrelenting desire to help his family back in

China. He solicited advice from several members of the board of the Houston Ballet with whom he had established strong and trusted relationships. They advised him to consider the stock market, which dumbfounded him; he'd had no exposure with the stock market while growing up in China. In fact, he recalled, since his parents never had money, they'd never even had a bank account.

Thus, he started from scratch and studied finance at the Australian Securities Institute with the plan to become a stockbroker, while continuing his career in dance. This meant rising at five in the morning for his daily ballet regime and then rushing to the stock exchange to arrive by eight. Cunxin's schedule was once again grueling; by the time he joined the rest of the company's dancers for afternoon rehearsals, he had already put in a full day's work. He retired from ballet at the age of thirty-eight and began the successful career transition from ballet to finance in 1999. His work ethic was astounding, and he ultimately became a senior manager at one of the largest stockbrokerage firms in Australia.

However, the financial field was not his passion. Ballet never truly left Cunxin, and he had a desire to return to the field that had given him his freedom. In 2012, he was given this opportunity by being appointed the artistic director of the Queensland Ballet. Once again, he embraced the creative roots that provided his resurrection from extreme poverty as a young boy. In considering his debut ballet, Cunxin chose *Cinderella*, which he had performed many times throughout his career. He asked his friend, mentor, and former Houston Ballet artistic director, Ben Stevenson, to teach the choreography, closing the circle of a lifelong friendship that had endured as many challenges as victories. In discussing his premier performance, he emotionally expressed that, to him, "*Cinderella* is a story full of hope, and I think hope is a beautiful thing in life. If one can bring hope, one can potentially have magic in life."

Cunxin's beginning was not grand in any way. At age thirty-eight, it seemed the only passion he knew would be snuffed out like a candle's flame due to his age. However, his life was enriched through each varied experience. He captured each twist and turn in his best-selling autobiography, *Mao's Last Dancer,* published in 2003 when he was forty-two. And at fifty-three, he was able to return to his greatest professional love—dancing. Against all odds, Cunxin successfully jumped out of the well into which he was born, and he is experiencing a rich life in the world above the hole in the ground.

> **From the depths of Communist China as a child, and persevering as an aging dancer, Li Cunxin claimed financial security and happiness after the age of fifty-three.**

Change is an Open Door

Even at first glance, Cunxin's sinewy, rock-hard dancer's body epitomizes his unbreakable and indomitable spirit. His childhood of limited foreseeable opportunities and poverty of surreal proportion appears not to have been the most fertile ground. And yet, the resiliency he learned from his parents' courage came to fruition in a series of remarkably unexpected paths that he traveled.

Culled from thousands, Cunxin was chosen as one of forty young people to join the national ballet academy in China. It was his first fortuitous opportunity. Though smaller and weaker than many of his peers, once he realized his uncultivated love of dance, he committed to give it all he had. He worked late into the evenings to perfect his leaps and turns. He rose early in the morning to jump up and down flights of stairs with heavy bags of sand tied around his legs to build strength. He latched onto this unexpected, unplanned opportunity with sweat, endurance, and resolve, ultimately opening the door to his destiny.

Li never sold his soul. Despite rising to become one of the foremost dancers in the world, being absorbed into the social circles of Houston a far distance from his upbringing, and ultimately making the decision to defect from his home country, he never forgot who he was or whence he came. He remained steadfast in his love, allegiance, and support for his family. The work ethic his parents and brothers instilled in him was, and continued to be, his North Star. Furthermore, when faced with the decision of providing for his budding family through a permanent departure from the work that he loved into the world of finance, he stayed true to his passion.

The story of Li Cunxin is much more than a rags-to-riches Horatio Alger story. The greatest takeaway for me is the thread of hope that, even today, weaves through every aspect of his life. He continues to inspire and motivate, not only through his words but also through his remarkable life and actions. Arguably, his most relevant contribution to the often entitled society in which we live is the constant reminder that our life is undoubtedly what we make it. He has indeed jumped out of the well into which he was born. He fully embraces the familiar verse: "To whom much is given, much is expected."

Alignment Lessons: Make It Real

- Never give up hope. "If you can bring hope, you can have magic in your life."

- It all comes down to how badly you want something.

- A person's work ethic creates his or her destiny.

- "When the heart weeps for what it has lost, the spirit laughs for what it has found."

Seize the opportunities life has to offer you. Embrace the changes. Have the courage to travel on roads less traveled, even though what is in front of you could be tough. Make it successful. Have determination and courage to kick down the brick walls in front of you and to go on and achieve bigger success than you ever thought possible.
—**Li Cunxin**

Diana Nyad
Roaring with Resilience

Isn't life about determining your own finish line? This journey has always been about reaching your own other shore, no matter what it is. That dream continues.
—**Diana Nyad**

Diana Nyad and her long-distance swimming records were world class even before she was catapulted onto the international stage in 2013. But it was her successful 110-mile swim in shark-and-jellyfish-infested waters—without a shark tank—that solidified her legacy. It was her fifth attempt to cross the stretch between Cuba and Florida, and she was sixty-four years of age. Her life's journey up until then had been one of mostly stoic courage in her attempts to overcome both internal and external demons.

Diana Nyad was born Diana Sneed in New York City in 1949. Her father, a stockbroker, and her mother divorced when she was very young. Her mother then married Aristotle Nyad, a Greek-Egyptian land developer, who adopted her. Her family relocated to Fort Lauderdale, Florida, where Diana joined her school's swim team at the age of ten. The team instructor, noticing Diana's skill, saw that great things were in store for her.

Unfortunately, Diana's home life was troubled. She has stated publicly that her stepfather molested her when she was eleven. From this horrific reality, Diana sought refuge. She found it in the water. She continued to excel in swimming and was enrolled in a private school where she could be coached and encouraged by the famed Olympian coach Jack Nelson. This male figure in her life also took advantage of her and began molesting her when she was fourteen years old. She seemed to channel the negative energy from these hardships into her swimming, as she won three Florida state high school championships during the years in which she was being violated. Her resiliency and determination were being solidified just as steel becomes forged in heat of the flame.

She continued to show tremendous promise, and she had dreams of swimming in the 1968 Olympics. However, again misfortune dealt a very hard blow. Due to a serious infection in her heart, she had to be bedridden for three months. When she was able to resume her training, she was so weakened that her strength and speed had been severely compromised. The first of her many dreams was snuffed before fully manifesting.

Diana attended Emory University for a brief period and then transferred to Lake Forest College, from which she graduated Phi Beta Kappa with degrees in both English and French. She also began to focus on long-distance events and continued to dominate in her field, competing throughout the world and shattering records. She set a speed world record in 1975 for swimming around the island of Manhattan in under eight hours. At this time, at the peak of her fitness level and at a relatively young age, she made her first attempt to swim from Cuba to Florida. She swam inside a 20 x 40 foot shark cage, but the rough seas and eight-foot swells pushed her off course. After being in the water for forty-two hours and swimming seventy-six miles, her team of doctors removed her from the raging ocean. She once said that she never wanted anything more than to complete the swim, and she was emotionally devastated at her failure. In 1979, on her thirtieth birthday, Diana entered into what was to be her last competitive swim. She subsequently set another world record for the 102.5-mile open-water swim from the Bahamas to Florida without a protective shark cage, breaking the distance records held by both women *and* men.

At this point, Diana thought her swimming career was over, and she embarked on another chapter in her life as a broadcast sports journalist. Over the course of the next thirty years she led a relatively normal life. She achieved success with a variety of programs, including *Wide World of Sports* and *One on One with Diana Nyad*. She wrote her first autobiography, *Other Shores*, and published a fitness book, *Basic Training for Women*. She was a frequent contributor to NPR's *All Things Considered* and wrote for numerous publications, including *The New York Times* and *Newsweek*.

Yet at sixty, something was still missing. She was middle-aged, single, and didn't have children. She was openly lesbian, but her long-term ten-year relationship had ended in 1994. Her father passed away in 1998 and her mother in 2007. She was an overachiever with a Type A personality who didn't have an overarching goal. Though she continued to push her physical self—often riding her bike over a hundred miles a day—she longed for something that would require *everything* she had to offer mentally, spiritually, and physically. She needed a big audacious goal, and she wanted to achieve it.

It was at this point in her life that Diana returned to the water. Starting over at age sixty, she began to rebuild her strong, athletic physique and to reclaim what she believed was her destiny. In 2011, some thirty-three years after her first attempt, she made the first of what would be five separate attempts to complete the journey between Cuba and Florida that she had previously tried to make when she was twenty-eight. Each tumultuous attempt was hindered either by rough weather; severe jellyfish stings, one of which left her temporarily paralyzed; or a life-threatening asthma attack that forced her to tread water for two hours while the doctors attempted to treat her. She once told a reporter, "I think I'm going to my grave without swimming from Cuba to Florida." But she did not give up. Many of her closest friends and supporters voiced considerable concern over her continued obsession to accomplish this feat, but she tried again and again. The grueling efforts cost hundreds of thousands of dollars and unfathomable pain and suffering.

On August 31, 2013, Diana stepped into the waters on the

shore of Havana, Cuba, to make her fifth attempt. A team of thirty-five specialists rode alongside her. As she swam, she wore a silicon mask, full body suit, and gloves and booties to prevent the venomous harpoon-like structures of the box jellyfish tentacles from penetrating her skin. Fifty-three hours later, on Labor Day, September 2, 2013, Diana Nyad achieved her dream, swimming the 110 miles between Havana and Key West.

Diana Nyad became the very first person to swim from Cuba to Florida without a shark cage or fins, doing so when she was sixty-four years old.

What More Do You Want?

In the spirit of full disclosure, I had never followed Diana Nyad's career. Her name and her story were entirely new to me when I began researching the late-in-life stories for this book. What particularly intrigued me about Diana was her unrelenting drive. By most people's standards, up until Diana accomplished this last goal, she had lived a very full life rich in accomplishments. In the 1970s, she was one of the best marathon swimmers in the world. She had broken speed records and distance records, but she had failed the one great endurance feat she coveted—the Cuba swim. Despite her thirty-year sabbatical from swimming, her unrelenting desire to clear that last hurdle never languished. It was there like a sleeping giant that when awakened would come back with a vengeance rivaled by nothing. This unwavering commitment to realize the dream she had as a young woman ensured she would, if nothing else, have no regrets in her attempts to achieve it.

I suspect marathon swimming can be quite lonely. It is hard to imagine fifty-four hours of immense solitude with the deafening crashing of the ocean waves and the pitch-black abyss beneath. A person is left to listen to her own voice. What this voice tells you is what you hear and believe. This emphasizes Diana's inspiring achievement of mastering her psyche. When Diana swims, she focuses her mind on repetitive thoughts, like a metronome keeping rhythm with her strokes. When she is in the pool, she will count off the laps in her head, in one of the four languages she speaks. When she is in the ocean, she alternates her counting with singing one of the eighty-five songs she has in her running playlist, ranging from Bob Dylan's "It Ain't Me, Babe" to John Lennon's "Imagine" to The Searchers' "Love Potion #9." She gives an entirely new meaning to mind over matter. That alignment of her mind, body, and spirit is her power and what unquestionably enabled her to succeed in her quest.

As Diana Nyad enters into what many may call the third chapter, it is doubtful she will have any regrets looking back at her life. She was able to silence whatever fears arose. She listened to the voice inside, nurtured and strengthened what it was whispering to her, and then released it to be heard like no other. It would have been easy for Diana to let go of the dream that had evaded her grasp earlier in her life. Instead, she deleted her doubts, negated the naysayers, and boldly took back what she believed was to be her destiny. Arriving at her Key West destination after this grueling final swim, she cemented her legacy as a life force representing bold dreams, persistent preparation, and fearless commitment.

Alignment Lessons: Make It Real

- Age is a mindset.

- From anger and personal tragedy can come tremendous determination. It is your choice.

- "Everyone has their share of heartache; it is up to us to find our way back to light."

- We can do whatever we set our minds to do.

- Commitment and perseverance makes us better people and our world a better place.

- Find a way.

- Our spirit is much stronger than our bodies. It is what is inside that makes us who we are.

I have three messages. One is we should never, ever give up. Two is you are never too old to chase your dreams. And three is—though it looks like a solitary sport, it takes a team.
—Diana Nyad

Janette Beckman/Getty Images

Frank McCourt
To and From the Ashes

*The sky is the limit. You never have
the same experience twice.*
—**Frank McCourt**

F rank McCourt's life had been a living testimony to survival and courage up until he was sixty years old. He was married to his third wife, was a public school teacher, and was barely eking out a living in New York City. His humble life was routine and far from extraordinary.

In the midst of the Great Depression, Francis "Frank" McCourt was born into extreme poverty in Brooklyn, New York. He had three younger brothers and a younger sister, who died a few months after birth. Given their dire financial hardships and seeking some sense of stability, the family moved back to their Irish roots. His father and mother were unable to find steady work in Belfast or Dublin, so they returned to his mother's native Limerick. Their financial situation continued to plummet, and they sank deeper into poverty. They lived in a rain-soaked slum, where Frank shared a bed with his parents and siblings. Food was scarce, and the potential of escape from the horrid situation seemed slim to nonexistent. His father spent days numbing his reality with alcohol, drinking away what little money they had. Frank's brothers, twins, died early in their childhood due to the squalor of their circumstances. Two more brothers were born not too long thereafter.

When Frank was only eleven, his father left home and set out to find work in the wartime factories of England. He found work, but he rarely sent back money to support the family. Eventually, his father abandoned the family altogether, which left his mother to rear her four surviving children—all on the edge of starvation—without any source of income. At thirteen, Frank's formal education ended when his school, the Irish Christian Brothers, rejected him. At fourteen, he was hired by the Limerick Post Office to deliver telegrams, and he also earned money delivering the *Irish Times*. While he used much of the money to help his family, he also saved some for his own dream: to return to America. He also stole bread and milk in an effort to provide for his mother and three surviving brothers. His childhood was anything but charmed, which would ironically help him fulfill his destiny.

In 1949, at the age of nineteen, using money he had saved from his odd post office job, Frank caught a boat to head back to New York. Through an incidental encounter on the ship, he met a priest who helped him find a room in which to stay and also aided him in finding a job at the Biltmore Hotel. This job enabled him to make about $26 a week, $10 of which he sent back to support his mother in Limerick. Two years later, Frank was drafted into the Korean War and stationed in Bavaria. Upon his discharge from the US Army, he returned to New York City, where he held a series of nondescript jobs on the docks, in warehouses, and in banks.

Taking advantage of the G.I. Bill and claiming that he was an avid reader and quite intelligent, Frank was able to persuade New York University to accept him. He was admitted on one year's probation, provided he maintained a B average. He graduated in 1957 from New York University with a bachelor's degree in education. Frank received a master's degree from Brooklyn College in 1967, and then he became a public school teacher. He taught in various schools in Brooklyn and Manhattan for the next thirty years.

After he retired from education, Frank decided to write about his life in Ireland. His first book, *Angela's Ashes*, was published in 1996 and received national acclaim. It became an instant success, selling more than five million copies. It also earned critical recognition, winning the National Book Critics Circle Award, the Los Angeles Times Book Award, the ABBY Award, and the 1997 Pulitzer Prize for Biography. Frank was sixty-four years old when he achieved fame as a writer. He went on to pen additional memoirs: *'Tis* in 1999, which picked up at the end of the previous book and focused on life as a new immigrant in America, and *Teacher Man* in 2005, about his experiences as a new, uncertain teacher in the public school system in New York City.

It is safe to say that Frank's life legacy did not fully manifest until he began writing. He died in New York City at age seventy-eight, fourteen years after the publication of his first book.

Frank McCourt became a Pulitzer Prize–winning author and highly regarded contributor to the world of literature all after the age of sixty-four.

How Badly Do You Want It?

Frank McCourt's Pulitzer Prize–winning memoir, *Angela's Ashes,* took the world by storm in 1996, the year it was published. When I first read it, the extreme poverty and unfathomable conditions in which Frank and his family lived in Ireland were hard to comprehend. Imagine living in a lean-to flat at the end of an unpaved road next to the only latrine in the slum. When the rains came, sewage and polluted water would rise up through the floor, flooding the home. There was no food other than what could be stolen from leftover rations from nearby restaurants. There was only one rain-soaked mattress for the *entire* family to share. Each child had a rig of rags, which they called clothes, and a pair of slit shoes, which did little to soften the hard rocks that dogged their swollen feet. Despite having to quit school at fourteen to provide for his family, Frank scrimped, salvaged, and stole enough money to pay for transport back to America. His spirit of determined will and desperate resiliency astounds.

In working with diverse school educators from Brooklyn and the Bronx to the Rio Grande Valley and throughout Central Texas, I have met many individuals whose stories rival Frank McCourt's. From rape, incarceration, parents fighting drug and alcohol addictions, gang-infested communities, to extreme government-subsidized poverty, these resilient representatives of the human condition also fought their way out of destitution. The common denominator was dire determination. They wanted out badly. They wanted a life different than the one they had known. It all comes down to that, doesn't it? Just how badly do we want to change the conditions in which we find ourselves?

The transformational impact an incidental encounter can have is present once again in Frank's story. Upon passage from Limerick to New York, Frank happened to meet a priest who served as his first anonymous angel guiding him on his new path. Through this random meeting, he had a place to stay and a job. It is my belief that the priest was purposefully placed on Frank's path to help him find his way. Each of us has hundreds, if not thousands, of incidental encounters in our lives. Most of the time, we do not pay attention to them, as we are so busy running on our hamster wheel that we don't take the time or interest to engage. Thankfully, Frank did.

Arguably, Frank's lasting legacy did not begin until he was sixty-four years old; however, his life and ultimately his memoir was a compilation of those sixty-four years. Without having lived the life he had lived, he would not have been awarded a Pulitzer Prize or an ABBY award or given distinction in the world of literature. Through his hardships came his glory. It is as if through his own living hell, he met himself and then introduced the world to that irrepressible individual. The beautiful Latin phrase *amor fati* loosely translates to "love of one's fate." Though Frank McCourt most certainly did not love the experience of his fated childhood and early life, he transcended the experiences of those formative years, realizing that even the suffering and loss in one's life can be shaped into something beautiful and good.

Alignment Lessons: Make It Real

- Incidental encounters can change your life.

- Your life is full of turns, each revealing fresh perspectives.

- One's legacy is not determined until the last breath is taken.

- Each experience offers new opportunities, each building upon the other. We must transcend and include these experiences to fully evolve and develop into the person we are to become in this life.

You feel a sense of urgency, especially at my advanced age, when you're staring into the grave.
—**Frank McCourt**

Ninfa Laurenzo
Autumn Season Success

*I don't look at the business in terms
of money. I look at it in terms of the
fulfillment that I've been able to give
myself and give to others.*
—Ninfa Laurenzo

There is probably not a single person who lived in Texas
from 1973 through the late 1990s who has not eaten at
Ninfa's. This famous chain of restaurants became iconic for
two reasons. The first was its unique Mexican fare that was
freshly made on the premises. The other was the bustling
woman brimming with energy and warmth who founded it,
Ninfa Laurenzo. Mama Ninfa, as she was known, was given
credit for introducing tacos al carbon—now known as fajitas—
to the United States. Instead of the typical tacos made from

ground beef, Mama Ninfa served succulent, chopped, char-grilled beef filet folded into soft, handmade flour tortillas. The novelty was the cornerstone on which Mama Ninfa built her successful empire.

Ninfa's stumble into fame and financial security was certainly not easy, instant, or without cuts and scrapes. It took her years of sweat equity, painful tragedies, and setbacks before she met success.

Maria Ninfa Rodriguez was born in the border town of Harlingen, Texas, in 1924 and reared in her Catholic family alongside her eleven brothers and sisters. On this small patch of farmland in the Rio Grande Valley, her values were established. Her father was a hard-working plumber, and her mother was a homemaker who either grew or raised the food her family ate and sold the rest. Maria Ninfa's childhood was modest, but she was anchored in her strong faith and the belief that in America anything was possible.

After she graduated from high school and Durham Business School in Harlingen, Maria Ninfa made a trip to Rhode Island where her twin sister, Pilar, was living. It was here that she met and married the love of her life, Domenic Thomas Laurenzo, whom she nicknamed D.T. He was a Rhode Island native of Italian descent and had a passion for life and baseball. His upbringing was in many ways the diametric opposite of her humble Hispanic background in south Texas, yet their belief in big opportunities and living life large was a common thread weaving their lives together. They were married in 1945 and had their first child a few years later. They were considering putting down their family roots in either Los Angeles or Houston. It was by a mere toss of a coin that they moved to Houston, Texas, in 1949.

The two budding entrepreneurs pooled their funds and courage to open the Rio Grande Tortilla Factory. For the next twenty years they would rise at 3:30 a.m. to roll out corn tortillas for local restaurants to serve. They worked sixteen-hour days to provide for their five children and to enable them to attend excellent private parochial schools. They believed in the value of education. As Ninfa's daughter later shared, her mother believed that education was the passport to opportunity.

The Laurenzos' tortilla factory prospered, and they were able to garner modest financial success, but they maintained a very humble lifestyle and even continued to live in their small-frame house next to the factory. Devout Catholics, they considered their lives blessed with their meager business opportunity as well as their healthy children. Maria Ninfa's life was rich and full by her standards and more bountiful than she had ever expected.

In 1969 her life took a dramatic turn. Her beloved husband of twenty-two years collapsed due to a cerebral hemorrhage and died in her arms. Ninfa was forty-five years old and suddenly a widow saddled with rearing five children single-handedly. Their once thriving factory was struggling, and they had taken on considerable debt. Ninfa would later say that she had been desperate at this point in her life. She once said, "I used to kneel down and pray in my walk-in closet. And one night, shortly thereafter, I dreamt that I had a little taco stand." Little did she know that her prayers and her dream would indeed become a reality.

Ninfa continued to rise at 3:30 a.m. to pour her energy into ensuring the factory ran smoothly. She raised her children with the fortitude and stalwart spirit that would become her legacy. It was her philosophy to just keep going, as she fervently believed that doing so was what D.T. would have wanted.

Despite her perseverance and hard work, in 1972 it became apparent that the tortilla factory was not sustainable. It was losing money, and she was faced with the expense of a mandatory update to the equipment to comply with new manufacturing regulations. At this juncture, Ninfa decided to turn the tortilla factory into a small restaurant. However, she did not have the money she needed to finish out the interiors, and the banks turned her down for a loan. She mortgaged her house, borrowed a few thousand dollars from a friend in Mexico City, and scraped together pots and pans from her own kitchen to use in the new restaurant.

She then divided the factory building in half, put ten tables and forty chairs in the front half of the building, leaving the back half of the restaurant to continue operating as a tortilla factory. Opening in July 1973, this quirky little building became the first Ninfa's restaurant. On the day it opened, she and four of her five children ran the restaurant, and the till held a mere $16. Amazingly, people flocked to this little restaurant, which sold an astounding 250 tacos al carbon on the first day! Though this initial restaurant unfortunately burned to the ground a few weeks later, it was quickly rebuilt, and the rest, as they say, is history.

Aside from the tacos al carbon, Ninfa's most famous dish

was her avocado-and-tomatillo green sauce, which she created on the spur of the moment when a customer asked for *salsa verde*. She was known for her resourcefulness and creative common sense. Ninfa was, in a word, plucky. She once said, "You don't learn everything from textbooks. Life teaches you. You just have to have common sense and be practical."

The reputation of Ninfa and her classic Mexican cooking, which she had learned from her mother, spread quickly, and before too long, her little dive of a restaurant attracted Hollywood stars, sports figures, musicians, and politicians who could not get enough of her warm, authentic flavors. In fact, former President George Bush and First Lady Barbara Bush often asked Ninfa to bring her food to Washington for the presidential family. Other notables also frequented Ninfa's. John Travolta had a private corner at the restaurant while he was filming *Urban Cowboy*, and he made several stops in Houston in his private plane to get Ninfa's food to go.

Over the years, the initial Ninfa's restaurant, located on Navigation Street in Houston, was so successful that they tripled the size of the restaurant and closed the tortilla factory. Customers flocked from all over Texas, and Ninfa left her first kitchen on Navigation to open a second location on Westheimer, also in Houston. She became an iconic figure to her patrons. With her squinty, twinkling eyes framed by her chestnut bouffant, she greeted and hugged her guests as if they were visiting her own home. Grown men, women, and children coveted their "minute with Mama Ninfa." She became a mecca for those needing a warm shoulder, a reassuring squeeze, or plain-spoken advice on anything from marital woes to financial road bumps. Her maternal spirit, as much as her Mexican fare, drew throngs of people from far and wide. It was her indomitable force that captivated thousands and made them feel like they were part of an extended family.

In just under a decade, by the time Ninfa was in her late fifties, she and her family had opened nine restaurants in the Houston area. Maria Ninfa Rodriguez Laurenzo was by this time a millionaire and the corporate founder of a $30 million-per-year business that served homespun, authentic Mexican food, loaded margaritas, and a healthy dose of customer-centered love to thousands of loyal patrons. Just eight years before, she was in debt, a recent widow, a single mom of five children, and was struggling on every front. The Ninfa's chain of restaurants would ultimately have fifty-one locations throughout Texas. She even opened a location in Germany.

Ninfa believed that God answered the prayer she asked so many years before in her closet. That taco stand became a hit and the go-to place for an entire generation. She never lived an opulent lifestyle. She believed in putting back into the business and continued to live modestly in her Houston suburban neighborhood. Ninfa also believed in giving back to her community and nation, which she believed had offered her the opportunities to create the life she and her family enjoyed. She served on numerous boards, including the John F. Kennedy Center for the Performing Arts, the University Cancer Foundation–M.D. Anderson Cancer Center, and the Houston Hispanic Forum.

The Ninfa's restaurant chain ultimately had to file for bankruptcy in late 1996, primarily due to expanding too rapidly and because some of the restaurant managers failed to adhere to the watchful eye and attention to detail for which Mama Ninfa was known. Regardless, Mama Ninfa was and still is revered for her spunk, tenacity, entrepreneurship, and, primarily, for her devotion to her employees and patrons, whom she viewed as extended *familia*. She remained gracious throughout this period and continued to count her opportunities as blessings.

When Ninfa was seventy-five, she underwent a mastectomy for breast cancer and promptly added this disease to her list of causes for which she worked to raise awareness. Her death two years later, in 2001, from bone cancer, was a loss felt by many whom she may never have known personally. At her memorial service, her children recalled her proudest moment. In 1984, she had been appointed by Vice President Bush as one of five goodwill ambassadors to welcome Pope John Paul II in Puerto Rico. As a devout Catholic, Ninfa was honored. Lest their mother be perceived as anyone other than the down-home, cheek-pinching "mama to all," her children reveled in recalling this story about one of her many trips to Rome: "Once, we went to Alfredo's in Rome, where fettuccine Alfredo was invented. Alfredo himself came to our table to toss our noodles. After he was done, he proudly set the bowl in front of Mama, who reached down into her purse and pulled out a bottle of Tabasco sauce." Mama Ninfa casually turned to her children and said: "I am who I am."

Mama Ninfa built a multimillion-dollar business from scratch and an institution revered by many generations, all after she had turned fifty.

The Power of Being Real

There is not a single person reading this who has not or will not face the death of loved ones in their lives. Most of the individuals highlighted in this book had unforeseen and untimely misfortune in their lives, and in each case, these setbacks served as catalysts for change. Mama Ninfa was no exception. At only forty-five years of age, she suddenly and tragically lost her husband, the love of her life. In addition, there was the scary reality that she had become the sole provider for five young children and was left with financial debt. The distinguishing characteristic was her unflinching decision to stoically move forward. She had grit. She had what my mother calls "the stuff," that powerful combination of gumption, capability, and chutzpah. Her fear did not paralyze her; it catapulted her to heights even she had not envisioned. She thrust her shoulders back, held her chin up, and powered onward.

Each of us will undoubtedly be given the opportunity to stand tall when facing obstacles. There is no such thing as life without a skinned knee. The individuals who move through life courageously and joyously have not necessarily been blessed with lives absent of hardship, rich only in success and prosperity. Such people have, however, made the choice to take the circumstances they've been handed and make them into something great. That is a universal truth; we can only control our attitudes, our behaviors, and our choices. We do not control all the experiences life will give to us, yet we do control *our* responses in thought, word, and deed. Mama Ninfa did not shy away; rather, she put her face to the wind and simply did what she had to do to provide for her family.

Mama Ninfa's charismatic style and contagious leadership capability was rooted in her authenticity. Simply put, she never tried to be anyone she was not. She remained true to her origins and to her natural personality, which manifested as an innate maternal instinct that extended far past her blood family and into the hearts of presidents, popes, and most of all her patrons. Authenticity was her power. She knew who she was, and she stayed firmly grounded in that knowledge. This is the secret sauce of all individuals who leave legacies. They build them from their true selves, not who they think they should be or are supposed to be by someone else's standards or rules. Mama Ninfa's true self was formed from her experiences, trials, and tribulations, and she ultimately created a lasting reputation built on a bedrock of an intense work ethic, gratitude for what she had been given, and a sacred responsibility to give back to her community and the world.

Alignment Lessons: Make It Real

- Count your blessings.

- Death is a part of life.

- Learn from every experience.

- Be resourceful, be practical, work hard, and do what you have to do.

- Treat everyone as extended family, as indeed we all are.

- Be who you are.

There is an attitude in Texas that makes you feel you can do anything you want to do. I admire so many women who have come out of Texas and done well. I like the image Texas brings to mind—that of bigness, of strength, of goodness.
—Ninfa Laurenzo

Stephen Shugerman/Getty Images

Kathryn Joosten
Carpool to Credits

*Some people in Hollywood think of me as
a model for dramatic midlife transitions:
suburban housewife to Emmy-winning
actress. But I never plotted a master
plan for following my dreams.*
—Kathryn Joosten

I fell in love with Kathryn Joosten's matter-of-fact, straight-talking characters on many television shows in the 1990s. Kathryn was known for her roles portraying as dry, crusty, and a bit eccentric older women, not unlike many aspects of the real Kathryn Joosten. She was new to me—and to the world for that matter—as she had only arrived in Hollywood a few years before, at the age of fifty-five. The road that brought Kathryn to television fame had been marred with potholes. Yet she had navigated the dips and ruts like a true professional and not only survived the journey but also found her pot of gold at the end of the trek.

Kathryn was born in Chicago in 1939, to Dutch-German parents. Her origin offers one explanation for her hard-headedness and saucy way of approaching life. There is little doubt that through being reared immediately following the Great Depression, in the era of grit and grindstone, when employment was often a luxury, Kathryn had learned to not shy away from the drudgery of hard work. From an early age, she had little fear, and she met life with a brassy, bold belief that what she set out to do, she would do—in spades.

When Kathryn was in her twenties, her mother passed away from cancer. While her mother was in the hospital, her deathbed confession to Kathryn was that she regretted not following her dreams. It was this life-changing moment that imprinted a vow on Kathryn's soul. She decided that she would not have the same regrets and that she would someday pursue her dreams. Her primary dream was to become an actress.

At this time, in 1963, Kathryn was just beginning a new career as a psychiatric nurse for disturbed teenagers. Through this difficult work, she met and married her husband, a psychiatrist in the same hospital. They settled down to a fairly well-to-do lifestyle in the suburbs of Lake Forest, Illinois, and Kathryn gave birth to two sons. Her life as a suburban house-wife and mother was embraced with vim and vigor, but she never let go of her dream to become an actress. She played the role of dutiful wife and adoring mother for almost twenty years, until, in 1980, her husband's extreme alcoholism prompted Kathryn to divorce him. As many women can relate, she found herself with two young boys to feed and rear alone and with virtually no current skills by which to provide for her family. This juncture reintroduced the opportunity to jump off the cliff and pursue her long-lost dream. Rather than continue a conventional lifestyle, Kathryn chose the avant-garde avenue of becoming an actress.

With two boys under her wing and the looming and sacred responsibility of their well-being, Kathryn stepped out into the foreign world of acting. She began by taking theatre classes at the Steppenwolf Theatre in Chicago. Next she tried her hand at regional performances in the area. Needless to say, these efforts did not pay the bills. To make ends meet and to provide all the necessities for her family, she held a wide array of odd jobs. She hung wallpaper, painted the interiors of the affluent set's mansions, and even worked as a salesperson for a Welcome Wagon company. At night, she continued to exercise her acting muscles, attempting to improve her overall skills. In 1991, she had her first break.

The Walt Disney Company was hosting a cattle-call audition for street performers for Disney World. After standing in line for more than five hours, Kathryn auditioned and won the part. She was soon to be a full-fledged, paid performer. She drove with her boys to Florida, where she could finally earn a living doing what she loved. Despite being positioned behind an adult arcade and tolerating rude tourists, she was happy and having the time of her life. Unfortunately, the position only lasted a short year, and Kathryn then took a job as a bartender. Her can-do spirit was bolstered by her confidence that she had the talent to make it as an actor. She also knew success hinged on perseverance and stick-to-itiveness. She soldiered on for two more years, eventually awakening to the reality that central Florida was not the mecca for acting. So she packed her bags, loaded the boys into her truck, and drove to Hollywood. She was fifty-six years old and had no agent, no contacts in the industry, and nowhere to live upon arrival.

A short five months later, Kathryn landed her first part. In 1995, she had two seemingly insignificant lines in the sitcom *Family Matters*. She became known as a middle-aged character actress with consummate comedic timing. Over the next six years, she appeared in numerous plays, six movies, eleven national commercials, two pilots, ten drama series, and more than twenty sitcoms. Her gravelly voice and dry, sassy temperament made her the ideal choice for roles ranging from mothers and grandmothers to Mrs. Landingham, the friend and personal secretary to Martin Sheen's President on *The West Wing*, which became an iconic character much like Nancy Kulp's administrative character Miss Jane to Mr. Drysdale on *The Beverly Hillbillies* from my childhood. It was this particular role that propelled her into the prominence for which she had worked so hard. The role gave her a way into weightier guest parts in other television series. Namely, she was lured onto the sets of *Spin City, The X-Files, Will & Grace, The Closer*, and *Reba*, to name only a few. Kathryn had arrived at the destination she had been driving toward for decades.

In 2004, she landed her final and most memorable television role as the multilayered Karen McCluskey, the neighborhood nemesis on the wildly popular *Desperate Housewives*. Though a protagonist known for persistent bickering and rabble-rousing ruckus, deep down she was a good woman full of love and past heartache. Audiences fell in love with her character—and her. She won two Emmy Awards for this role, and was nominated for two additional Emmys and a Screen Actors Guild Award, arguably two of the most coveted confirmations of a person's talent in the industry.

At seventy, Kathryn was in discussion with the famed Lily Tomlin to star in a *Desperate Housewives* spinoff. Both actresses were beyond their prime years, yet their individual and collective talents defied the Hollywood obsession with youth. Unfortunately, later that year, Kathryn was diagnosed with a recurrence of lung cancer, which had initially besieged her in 2001 after a forty-five-year cigarette-smoking habit. She endured surgery and four rounds of chemotherapy, and in 2010 she was pronounced cancer-free. She used her lung cancer experience to teach others the dangers of cigarette smoking, even discussing the experience during a guest appearance on *The Bold and the Beautiful*.

Ironically, twenty days after her character Karen McCluskey died of brain cancer in the final episode of *Desperate Housewives*, Kathryn succumbed to the disease that had plagued her for eleven years. She left a band of fans who are as inspired by her spunky snubbing of a town's ruthless rules around youth and beauty as they are by her theatrical talents. Through her life, Kathryn encourages us to disregard the conventional structures that bind so many and seek vocations that liberate our juiciest creativity.

Kathryn Joosten left a middle-class conventional lifestyle, followed her passion, arrived in Hollywood at age fifty-five, and won her first of two Emmy Awards when she was sixty-nine.

It Is Never Too Late

Kathryn Joosten defied the odds. It is hard to imagine voluntarily leaving a life of conventional comfort, picking up your family, and moving halfway across the United States to become a street performer at the age of fifty-two. Nothing was certain, certainly not success or longevity of position. There was little, if any, security in this drastic move. Amazingly, this blind bolt was only the first of many brave vaults in Kathryn's life. She leapt to Hollywood just three years later with little more than a hope and a dream. One might argue *now*, what more was needed? Yet at the time, it is hard to fathom the enormous risk she took.

Kathryn was no-nonsense in most areas of her life. She was not afraid to sweat. She had little time for pretense or falderal. Her work ethic and her words were Midwestern matter-of-fact. She valued the "little people" on set and counted the crew as a few of her closest compadres. This straightforwardness in life and about the business of acting served her well. She was never mired in the mirage of fame. Acting was a job to Kathryn, albeit one that was highly fulfilling and undisputedly her calling. When Kathryn surrendered to the dream, she became authentically aligned. She loved what she did, she was good at it, and it was tied to something much greater than herself. Yet, she never became intoxicated by the spirits of celebrity. She knew who she was, and she never forgot.

Fear was certainly present, but it was never the trump card. Her dream trumped her fear. Her drive squelched the little voices that whispered, "What are you doing?!" Her distinction was her unyielding quest to continue, regardless of the possible perils. She wanted it badly enough to take enormous risks. Her key was that she anchored that risk in the knowledge she had gained in Florida; she knew she had what it took to be successful—raw talent. That self-awareness and objective assessment of her abilities increased her appetite. Had she any doubts about her competency, the risks would have been pure folly. She believed in herself.

The final lesson we can learn from Kathryn's story lies in her profound humility in admitting the mistakes of her past. She had smoked for more than forty-five years, and this led to her ultimate physical demise. Like an alchemist, she took that heinous habit and the insidious cancer it caused and used it to communicate thoughtfully and retrospectively about her life and her choices, and to caution others. She was not embittered, but she *was* angry. She was angry at many, yet mostly herself. She was open and honest in her feelings. She did not hold back due to false pride or arrogant defiance. She owned her mistake and through her vulnerability displayed triumphant courage. This trait of sheer grit was evidenced throughout her life. Kathryn's unvarnished legacy is one of courageous will heartened by humor.

Alignment Lessons: Make It Real

- It is never too late to pursue your dreams.

- "For those who are afraid: jump off the board. Get in the water. You can always get out."

- Be real. Not everyone is going to like everyone. If you are true to yourself, and you are kind to others, the rest will take care of itself.

My fans are people . . . youngsters who look at me as a grandmother. People who wanna make a change, people who are on the edge of saying this is not the life I chose and I wanna do something about it.
—Kathryn Joosten

Giorgio Armani
The Calm Couturier

*Never in my wildest dreams did I
entertain the idea that I would become
a fashion designer.*
—**Giorgio Armani**

The name Armani is synonymous with serene sophistication and style. For many, wearing an Armani gown or suit signifies having "made it" and serves as the signal of success for corporate tycoons and the Hollywood set alike. Giorgio Armani has established himself as comparable to Coco Chanel and Yves Saint Laurent as a fashion icon delivering uniquely timeless fashion designs to the world. His empire has expanded over the years, and its value was stated at well over $10 billion at the close of 2013. What is surprising about Giorgio's rise to fame in the fashion industry is that it was not destined nor a childhood dream. In fact, at one point Giorgio went to medical school with the plan of becoming a country doctor to save the lives of the impoverished. How the thread of his life wove from a humble childhood to global fashion icon is a colorful tapestry of serendipitous encounters and events.

Giorgio's life has not always been gilded and glamorous. He was born in Piacenza, a small town about forty miles southeast of Milan, in 1934. He was the second of three children who were reared during the horrors of World War II. His humble upbringing was clouded by the constant air raids and the deaths of many of his friends from the Allied bombings. As a child, he sought refuge outside his realities, and found sanctuary at the local cinema. He has said that he fell in love with the idealized beauty of the Hollywood stars. It was quite foreign to his dreary drab world.

At an early age, Giorgio became curious about human anatomy, an interest that has served him throughout his life. This fascination initially led to three years of studying medicine at the University of Piacenza. His parents were highly influential in persuading him into this field of study, despite Giorgio's ongoing interest in cinema and the visual arts. He was required to serve in the Italian military, so he took leave from his studies and enrolled in the service. He served in the Verona military hospital as a medical assistant for three long years. This experience shaded his perspective of becoming a physician, and rather than return to medical school, he dropped out. A friend landed him a position in a local department store in Milan named La

Rinascente. He served as a sales clerk in the men's department and also helped put together window displays, which were both ambitious and atypically represented products that the typical Italian consumer could not afford. Due to a departmental restructuring, Giorgio's supervisor transferred him to the Office of Fashion and Style. This functional area was commonly known within the organization as the "no-man's land" of the department store, where Giorgio had virtually nothing of consequence to do. This unlikely move provided the first blank canvas on which his talents would emerge.

Through this experience, he learned the importance of fabric, texture, and the melding of the two to create art. He also gained a heightened appreciation for the manner in which consumers respond to a fashion design, what appeals to them, and why. After seven years of learning what many may now call the basic principles of the fashion business, his manager encouraged him to apply for an assistant's position opening under textile magnate Nino Cerruti, for a new fashion line he was launching. When Giorgio recounts this interview process, it is astounding how this next step took place. Mr. Cerruti threw a pile of textile materials in front of him, and asked him to pick what he liked. As fate would have it, Giorgio picked what Mr. Cerruti also favored and landed the job! While holding this position, Giorgio fell in love with textiles. The richness of color, texture, and the movement of fabric on the human anatomy are the cornerstones of his style. These values were seeded through this initial experience with Mr. Cerruti. Giorgio's talents began to take root.

He began to freelance, offering opinions and designs to other manufacturers, while continuing to work at the Cerruti Company. It was during this time that he met Sergio Galeotti, an architectural draftsman nine years his junior, who would have a profoundly transformational impact on his life. Their friendship marked the beginning of a personal and professional collaboration that lasted for many years. Sergio recognized and encouraged Giorgio's immense talents. Through intense persuasion, he finally enticed Giorgio to leave his secure $40,000-per-year position to launch his own design office. The year was 1973, and Giorgio Armani was thirty-nine years old.

Armani went out on his own, with little more than his creativity, his drive, a pittance in the bank, and a partner by his side. This risky period propelled Armani into the fast lane of fashion houses, and the international press began to recognize his potential importance to the industry. With Sergio Galeotti managing his finances and the operational aspects of his business, he was free to draw and develop his own style and expand his creative reach. At age forty-two, he was ready to devote the majority of his energy to his own label, and in 1975, he and his Sergio founded Giorgio Armani S.p.A. in Milan, Italy. In October of that same year, he presented his first collection of men's ready-to-wear. A women's line followed quickly thereafter, also under his own name. A sobering fact was that in 1976, when both lines were introduced, the combined total sales were only $90,000. Despite the modest figure, his clothes were pronounced revolutionary and his color palette introduced an almost Zen subtlety to the market. And as importantly, Giorgio Armani believed in what he had to offer and his overall creative vision for how he wanted to contribute was crystal clear.

Still, Armani's rocket had not quite lifted off the ground. When Sergio and Giorgio first launched the company in 1975, they boasted a whopping working capital of only $10,000 and could only afford one employee, a student who worked as the receptionist. Yet their entrepreneurial enterprise was established, and their drive indisputable. Though Giorgio's designs had gained in popularity and were wildly sought after in Europe, they didn't take hold in America until 1980. Thanks to Richard Gere's sexy physique in the movie *American Gigolo*, Armani's form-fitting, tailored suits and sophisticated color palette were introduced to America. The ongoing love affair between Giorgio Armani and the big screen continued. Soon, Hollywood flocked to Armani, and stars from Michelle Pfeiffer and Jodie Foster to John Travolta and Annette Bening clamored to wear his designs. With Tinsel Town as the fuel, his small ember of a company finally took flame.

As his business continued to flourish in the 1980s, Giorgio's clothing lines moved into the corporate arena and became the power suits and symbols of success for the upwardly mobile crowd. Unfortunately, it was during this exciting high-growth period that Giorgio suffered an untimely and tragic personal and professional loss. His business partner and friend for ten years, Sergio Galeotti, died of complications from leukemia at only forty years of age. This heartbreak would become another defining moment of Giorgio's life.

The creative right brain, Giorgio was soon to prove to the world that he could also be an enterprising executive who could make hard calls and strategic decisions. The Armani brand extended beyond his neutral, well-constructed tailored creations and broadened to include other product offerings, ranging from eyeglasses and cosmetics to watches and home goods and even book publishing. New clothing lines and labels were launched to wide public appeal. At the same time, the Guggenheim Museum in New York hosted an exhibition of Armani's work, a first for a living designer. With average attendance of 29,000 people a week, the show featured Armani's evening wear for women, which, although one of the designer's strong areas, was not even his main claim to fame.

Over the past twenty years, Giorgio, now seventy-nine, has shown no sign of slowing down. His business is a family business. His sister Rosanna works at Armani as do two of his nieces, Silvana and Roberta. Recently, he has partnered with a Dubai developer to build two luxury hotels, one in Milan and another in Dubai's Burj Khalifa, the tallest building in the world. His enterprise stands today as one of the few remaining independent, privately owned companies in its sector, with a proven business strategy that has capitalized on the worldwide power and potential of the Armani brand name. The company Giorgio has built is a mirror of himself: enterprising, lean, chic, and forward thinking. With double-digit growth in his business in 2013 and a net worth of well over $10 billion, Giorgio Armani has proven that there is life after middle age. He emerged from potential middle-age complacency as a part-time store clerk and freelance designer to become a global fashion icon. He seems to apply his philosophy of fashion—that "it is about evolution and moving forward"—to his life, as well.

Giorgio Armani left his life as a back-room designer at age forty-three to launch his company with little more than his drive and raw talents. At seventy-nine, he has established global prominence in the industry and has a net worth of over $10 billion.

Making the Leap in Partnership and Collaboration

Giorgio Armani is beloved by his clients, respected by his peers, and revered by his family. Though today he would be considered part of the rich and famous, his life has not been without challenge or heartache. He could have chosen a life of mediocrity in Milan working in back rooms supporting others' dreams, yet there were forces at work designing a detour. The unexpected meeting and connection with Sergio put his ultimate destiny in motion. Sergio had confidence in Giorgio's talents. He buoyed him through the rough waters of freelancing design work and ultimately the launching of their initial business. Sergio's role in nurturing their fledging entrepreneurship was central to their ultimate success. In addition, Giorgio was humble enough to accept the support and embrace the tenuous proposition. They held fast. Together, they persevered, riding the turbulent tides of the fashion industry. Their partnership was one cemented in trust, and over time it glistened with Giorgio's gratitude. Sergio was the free spirit who became the energizing force behind the budding designer. As Giorgio would recall, "He woke me up from a sort of torpor, from the little life in which I was living." Their union was the magic mojo.

When tragedy struck and Sergio was taken, at what many would consider a premature age, Giorgio's life crumbled. Not only was Sergio integral to Giorgio's life, given the critical role he had played in running the company, many thought the business would not survive. Admittedly, Giorgio has said it was the single most difficult time in his life. Rather than wither and wallow in self-pity, Giorgio rallied and with his vision as the compass, he persevered. It took guts. Almost defiantly, he bucked up and, rather than let his business dwindle and dry up, he expanded. This moxie became a trademark for Giorgio. Rather than cave under the pressure, he chose to channel the adversity into courage and steadfastness.

One aspect of Giorgio Armani's life that particularly resonates with me is his commitment to his family and his inner circle of friends. His loyalty and ongoing inclusion in his life and business is notable. Many, when they hit the "big time," move away from family and seek new friends. Giorgio has taken his friends and family into his fold, teaching them the business and generously sharing his success and ongoing experiences with them. They collectively stretch and grow to extend their reach into diverse expressions of his creativity. His seminal contribution as a forward-thinking creative designer and entrepreneur has been established. Yet it is his legacy as a generous and inclusive uncle, brother, and teacher to his family that will resonate long after he is gone.

Alignment Lessons: Make It Real

- Individuals are placed in our lives for a reason.

- Friends and supporters are critical to one's success.

- Stay true to your heart and the design it wishes to create.

- Stay connected to the world and listen to what it needs.

- Diversify. Have the courage to take the risk and anchor it with what you know to be true.

- Think forward. Never dwell in the past; the past is the past.

I love things that age well, things that don't date, that stand the test of time, and that become living examples of the very best.
—Giorgio Armani

Wally Blume
The Ice Cream Man

---

*We thank God daily—not only for His
blessing on our business—but for what
He's done in our lives.*
—Wally Blume

When I was growing up, when one made reference to the
ice cream man, I always thought of the familiar melodic
music that came from the colorful truck as it meandered its
way through our neighborhood. Now, after learning about this
story, whenever I think of the ice cream man, I will also think
of Wally Blume. Wally Blume's success in the ice cream business is unparalleled. You may not know his name, yet you have
undoubtedly run across his trademark flavor, Moose Tracks®,
which is a sinful swirled combination of Moose Tracks® Fudge,
peanut butter cups, and vanilla ice cream. Amazingly, his wildly

successful business, which now enjoys well over $100 million in annual retail sales, was started in 1996 when Wally Blume was sixty-two years old.

Wally Blume's life and career up until this point will sound strangely familiar to many. He was reared in a middle-class family in Indianapolis, where his father was an employee of General Motors. His mother and father also owned and managed apartment buildings. Wally's parents emphasized hard work, and they expected Wally to help carry the load of the family business. After school, when many of his friends were playing baseball or goofing off, Wally was expected to clean apartments, cut grass, and help with the household chores. Discipline and a solid work ethic were ingrained in him. Though he may have disdained it at the time, these characteristics would serve him well throughout the rest of his life.

After high school, Wally went on to college and earned a degree in economics from Purdue University. Upon graduating in 1962, he landed his first job at the Kroger Company as a comanager of a grocery store in Indianapolis. He made an annual salary of $5,000, and to earn this sum, he worked sixty-hour weeks, including nights and weekends. It was incredibly difficult work, but it was an excellent experience. He learned the business basics: how to lead and manage people; how to hire and fire employees; and how businesses work and make money. There were strict rules and regulations within the Kroger Company, but just as in his childhood, he realized the necessity of rules and associated structure in a business. His bosses took notice of Wally's work ethic as well as his competitive nature. He always wanted to be on top. When there was an opportunity for him to shine or to excel, he took full advantage of it. This caught the store manager's eye, and in time, Wally earned his first promotion.

Wally stayed with his initial employer for the next two decades and worked his way through the corporate maze. He was running on the proverbial corporate hamster wheel when, in the mid-1980s, Kroger needed to cut numerous middle-management positions. Wally's job was eliminated. He immediately found another position, this time working for the largest dairy in Michigan, Country Fresh. He was put in charge of sales and marketing for milk and ice cream. Through this position, he met hundreds of contacts who bought and sold ingredients and packaging for ice cream. Building this network would prove to be vitally important to him long-term. When one of his connections passed away, his position as an independent broker was left open, and this spelled opportunity for Wally. He had always wanted to be his own boss, and now was his chance. The small ice cream ingredient company he represented allowed him to market creative and original flavors, which he loved. Unfortunately Wally's utopia did not last long. The small manufacturer he represented was bought by a large conglomerate that was struggling to grab additional market share. Wally's infamous wake-up call came when the company began to introduce strange flavors of ice cream, such as tomato and guava. Wally was not aligned with where this company was heading, so he decided to leave. He'd been in the business for more than thirty years when he made the brave decision to jump from the perceived security of the corporate nest and see if he could fly.

Wally and his partner began to create their own unique flavors of ice cream. The first flavor was created in 1988—a decadent concoction of Moose Tracks® Fudge, peanut butter cups, and vanilla. They named it Moose Tracks®, in homage to a miniature golf attraction near their first customer's dairy and his partner's enchantment with the state of Alaska. This combination was a confectionery coup. When introduced, Moose Tracks® began to outsell even vanilla and swept like an icy avalanche through the nation. By 1995, these enterprising entrepreneurs knew they had a hit on their hands.

It was at this juncture that Wally came to another fork in his road. He had always wanted to run his own business, yet he never had the wherewithal to make it happen. Looking back, when he was in his thirties and forties, Wally had toyed with going into a number of entrepreneurial ventures, including becoming an owner of a cheese broker franchise. But the pieces had never fully come together and, thus, he had resigned himself to a long corporate career working for someone else. Since Moose Tracks® had become an unexpected hit, he realized he had the opportunity *and* the product to finally start his own business.

In 2000, when he was sixty-two, he mortgaged his house and every other asset he could to buy out his partner and start fresh. That year, he launched Denali Flavors®, Inc. The name was an ongoing tribute to the state of Alaska, and he'd chosen it to continue to build upon the brand. Wally's vision was to create, market, and license unique ice cream flavors and dessert concepts for independent regional dairies to offer as competitive products to the large national dairy brands. This approach is quite tricky and where Wally's lengthy experience serves as a significant differentiator. Denali Flavors® can't actually "own" a flavor formulation. They can, however, own the name, the logo, and continue to protect their strong market penetration and sustainable quality by producing their own ingredients to be included in the manufacturing process. This unique approach has led Wally Blume's company to market more than forty unique flavors. And though Denali Flavors®' financial success cannot be made public, the flavors they market are stated to generate in excess of $100 million a year in retail sales through their related products. The company continues to expand through use of these flavors in cakes, cookies, and other ice-cream novelty products.

Wally and his wife, June, are devout Christians and have professed their faith regularly in tandem with their business. On the *700 Club* television program, Wally Blume stated, "The goal for our business is to fund the gospel." They believe in this mission, and support their religious convictions through a variety of ministries. One ministry that touches a diverse number of nonprofit organizations is their 10,000 Scoop Challenge. For every single free scoop of Moose Tracks® eaten, they donate $1 to a worthy beneficiary. Denali Flavors® has hosted these events in various locations to benefit notable organizations, such as The Salvation Army. This is just one example of how Wally Blume ties his business to something much greater than his own personal success.

From my perspective, Wally Blume's life epitomizes my definition of alignment. He most certainly loves his work, and he is clearly good at it. But the secret sauce for Wally Blume is in that last pillar: his work is tied to something much greater than himself.

Blooming When and Where Planted

Wally Blume is an ordinary guy. He had an average, middle-class, American upbringing, and he was fortunate enough to go to college and get a job upon graduation. He could have chosen to stay on a conventional path of predictable plenty; however, something spurred him to take the leap into the world of entre-preneurship. Wally chose to embrace the risk of possible failure to become the master of his own destiny. He always had the dream of being his own boss and building his own company. At the late age of sixty-two, it is hard to fathom the courage he mustered to mortgage all that he had accumulated to pursue this dream. Courage anchored in faith became his rudder, his stabilizer, and his driving force.

Many of us have dreams, and many of us may feel limited in our capacity to pursue them. We may feel financially hindered or psychologically paralyzed by fear, and thus we stymie ourselves into stagnation. Often, we choose to stay in our safe zone and continue along the path most traversed by others. There is a façade of contented comfort staying amidst the crowds on the moving sidewalk of life. It can be scary to jump the barricade to walk against the flow. Undeniably, when we decide to jump into the pool of uncertain outcomes, the litmus is almost always the answer to how badly we want "it." Wally wanted "it." "It" to him was to become his own boss, fueled by his steadfast belief that he could create something unique and transformative to the industry he knew so well. Yes, he faced an uncertain endgame, but he was willing to bend into formidable wind to pursue it.

Wally stayed in the game he knew. His industry knowledge told him what levers to pull. He knew where the uncovered bases were and where there were gaps to be filled. Having this experience was critical. Going out on one's own without experiential knowledge of a chosen field could be perceived as folly. The learning curve in any industry can be steep and greased with crafty competitors. Yet Wally's familiarity with his industry, coupled with his passionate work ethic, were vital to his success. In addition, over the years he had built long-standing relationships with people who championed his growth. Though it is not insurmountable to completely re-invent oneself late in life, in Wally's case, his background served him well.

Finally, the most inspiring aspect to Wally's late-blooming success is his conviction, passion, and commitment to a cause greater than himself. Wally believes he has a hallowed responsibility to fund charitable efforts that represent his Christian calling. He donates to, sponsors, and advocates for organizations serving those less fortunate. He is generous in thought, word, and deed, and believes the overarching purpose for his business is primarily to fund these philanthropic intentions. Regardless of the chosen cause, having our vocation and our lives tied to something greater than ourselves fosters evergreen energy. When we have our professions and career aspirations tied *solely* to the accumulation of wealth, power, status, or fame, we diminish our power. In addition, we most certainly will experience burnout and ultimately peter out due to lack of unadulterated purpose.

Wally Blume took a calculated risk. He followed his intuition and began again at the age of sixty-two. Almost twenty years later, he has churned a rich, sweet autumn season for his life. Wally Blume is fully and sweetly aligned.

Alignment Lessons: Make It Real

- Do what you love! Have FUN in life and in work.

- Know and understand your business and what drives it.

- Realize that businesses need structure. Metrics and accountability are important.

- It is never too late to pursue your dream.

- Keep it simple. Use common sense.

- Tie your life and your business to a power and purpose greater than yourself.

It doesn't take a Rhodes Scholar to understand that Moose Tracks® Fudge and peanut butter cups in vanilla ice cream are going to outsell tomato ice cream every day of the year.
—Wally Blume

Afterword

The impetus for this book is tied to autobiographical tendrils. I left the perceived security of a corporate leadership position earlier than most and experimented in other leadership roles in two other publically traded corporate cultures prior to launching my own entrepreneurial venture. As of the publication of this book, I have not married nor do I have biological or adopted children. Make no mistake: societal pressures abound by choosing this less-traveled road. Professional expectations, typically measured by wealth accumulation, titles, trappings, and power, elevate with age. When an individual detours from the familiar, eyebrows lift and heads cock. False judgments are made. Yet, over the course of this most recent chapter in my life, I have also observed those who have deviated from the routine of a conventional life can become curious and sometimes enviable examples of success. Also, increasingly, what used to be viewed as an exception to the rule has become much more commonplace. Mid- to late-life changes may be due to a person's choice, like mine; yet more often than not, these shifts are attributed to the involuntary consequences of age, reduced relevance of a person's skill or experience, the depressed economic climate, or the outright obsolescence of a person's chosen industry. Then, like the subjects in this book, we are given the opportunity to start over in the last few decades of our time on earth.

In reflecting on the lives of these late bloomers, there is much to learn from their example. They have proven that it is never too late to create the life we want or to contribute in a manner that makes our heart sing. Until we have taken our last breath, we have the ability to establish lasting legacies and to make an enduring impact on the world. Regardless of our age, there are a few powerful guideposts we can glean from these stories.

Define Success on Your Terms

Success is individual. It is aligning who you really are inside with how you choose to contribute in the world. It cannot be limited in scope by a mere accumulation of tangible objects. Much like happiness, it is not defined by money, status, or power—real or imagined. Despite the ever-growing preoccupation with wealth and opulence and the stark reality that money is vitally important for our existence on earth, it is not the only metric for success. Like a barometer, financial reward can serve as a gauge of the weather, but it does not make or control the rain.

Success is not stagnant. It evolves and changes shape and scope as we evolve. Our definitions of success and what is important to us will invariably change as we move through life. What may have been our criteria for having "made it" when we were in college may change as we enter the last half of our lives. For many, this may sound like a rationalization of not having achieved certain goals from youth; however, I prefer to believe this is a clarifying process of what truly is important to us given our limited time on earth.

As unique as we are, so are the definitions of success. Each of us writes our own definition of success from the corners of our soul. Success comes from within. It is not awarded from the outside. One person may find their seat of success through painting images from their memory, like Grandma Moses, while another defines success as cradling grieving families as they navigate death, like Dorothy Winn. By staying in alignment with who you really are, and how you make meaning in the world, you will find and create your own benchmarks for success. They are not defined by corporate America, the expectations of society, by money, power, affluence, or influence. We all have the opportunity to define success for ourselves and the revered responsibility to sit in our own unique seat of authentic power.

Alignment Lessons: Make It Real

- What do *you* want?

- About what are you most passionate?

- How do you define success?

- How have you let others define success for you?

- Are your goals aligned with your true and most authentic self?

Incidental Encounters Are Not Incidental

In my first book, *Is This Seat Taken? Random Encounters That Change Your Life*, I share vignettes of chance meetings of individuals whose lives are changed without them realizing it. The book's foundational premise is that we are all part of an integral dance through life. We are part of a collective consciousness and our lives are a giant community whose streets intersect, and whose incidental rendezvouses affect our individual and collective experiences. These encounters create ripples in our pool of life and can start a wave of change often invisible to either party at the time. The only prerequisite to take advantage of these encounters is to be present in that moment. We must be awake and engaged. Just like when many door prizes are given away, we must be *present* to win!

Every single person's life has been affected by incidental encounters. Many may never know how these random interactions have changed the course of their journey; however, many do. Harland Sanders's life turned a distinct corner when he was picked up by a total stranger who ultimately offered him a job pumping gas. As he sailed back to America, Frank McCourt serendipitously met a priest on the ship's deck who helped him find a place to live upon arrival in New York City. Grandma Moses's initial paintings were discovered by an amateur art collector while on a business trip to Hoosick Falls. None of these fateful interactions were planned, but they had profound impact on each of these lives.

The same is true for us. Our lives are peppered with thousands of incidental interactions. These serendipitous exchanges can and do make imprints on our minds and hearts; and they can change our lives. We never know who, what, when, where, or how a person will cross our path and the potential cascade of events that meeting may initiate. We have to stay open, curious, and awake. We have to take our noses out of our smartphones and engage with those around us. When we do this, we open the door to potential, to opportunity, and to the miracles these individuals can spark in our lives.

Alignment Lessons: Make It Real

- What seemingly insignificant moment have you let pass without recognizing what it might have to offer?

- Have you ever been an "incidental encounter" in someone else's life? What impact did it have on you?

- What "chance meeting" has altered your perspective on life?

- What change can you make in your daily life to become more present in the moment?

We Always Have the Power of Choice

We do not control most of what happens in and around our lives. The economy will continue to fluctuate. The provision of healthcare for the masses will become increasingly strained, expensive, and inaccessible. Age discrimination will not go away overnight, if ever. There will probably not be much Social Security left when it comes our time to collect the benefits. Life's ups and downs will always resemble the ticker tape from an EKG machine: up, up, down; up, up, down. These peaks and valleys are the rhythm to which we keep time, and no one is immune to the constant cadence of life's challenges.

Yet we do have control over three basic things. We *can* control our ABCs. We can control our attitudes, our behaviors, and, most importantly, our choices. How we *choose* to deal with the curveballs defines who we are. At the root of our life's story, there is one basic truism: we own it. No one else does. The harsh reality is that no one *owes us* anything. Not our corporate employers, not the government, and not our various relationships in life. Sure, it would be great if we got everything we think we deserve in life. Yet, again, we do not control any of this. Nothing, nada, zilch. Welcome to the world of "life is not always fair." How we ultimately respond to these inequities and other occurrences is what creates our reality.

Take a look at our examples: Harland Sanders went bankrupt not once but *twice* before ultimately founding Kentucky Fried Chicken. Grandma Moses buried five of her ten children in their infancy, and Jacquie Qualls lost her long-standing job at age sixty-two, without enough financial security to retire. Every single person highlighted in this book has faced horrific challenges, ranging from raging alcoholism and bankruptcy to cancer and loss. Each person could have made different and perhaps easier choices that would have taken their lives in another direction.

Ultimately, we write our own stories. Each one of us has his own sack of rocks; what distinguishes us is how we carry the load. Giving up, caving in to the comfort of inertia, or believing the hand we've been dealt is the only game we can play seals our fate. We have the gift of free will, which is one of the most important privileges of our lives. We have the ability to choose the direction we want to go, despite where we find ourselves in life. We have the option to resign ourselves to a fate we believe has been predetermined; or we can take the reins and choose to pursue and create the life we want. Viktor Frankl wrote *Man's Search for Meaning*, which remains one of my favorite books and, at a very young age, transformed the way I look at the world. He wrote about his experiences in a Nazi concentration camp and explored the psychological effects that being completely dehumanized had on his fellow prisoners: "Everything can be taken from a man but one thing: the last of human freedoms—to choose one's attitude in any given set of circumstances, to choose one's own way." The power to choose never leaves us, regardless of the circumstances.

Alignment Lessons: Make It Real

- How are you using your gifts today?

- What choices are you making today?

- What guides you: your passions or life's inertia?

- What brings you bliss?

If We Are Alive, We Have a Purpose

Years ago, while I was recovering from surgery, I remember lamenting to my father about wanting to find my purpose in life and wondering if I even had a purpose. My father's response in a very matter-of-fact tone was, "You have one, otherwise you would be dead." Though it never occurred to me that I could have died at that time, his point was nonetheless direct and hard hitting. As long as we are alive, we have a reason for being here. I am a believer that we are here in earth school to teach one another, to learn from one another, and to serve each other, with love as the magic glue binding us together. *How* we do this differs for each individual and may change throughout our lives. We each are on our own individual journeys to contribute and serve at our highest potential. The wise quotation attributed to Joseph Campbell, sums up the "hero's journey" we are each traveling: "*We must be willing to let go of the life we planned so as to have the life that is waiting for us.*" Our call to "let go" may come at any time in our life and, as we have learned through these inspiring stories, our charge is to muster the courage to pursue our dreams at whatever stage in life we find ourselves.

The magic key that unlocks our potential is to dive deeply into who we really are as our most authentic self, and then reveal how we want to contribute in the world. Each person highlighted in this book did just that. They tapped into their distinctive talents and then proceeded to uniquely share these gifts with the world. From ballet dancer Li Cunxin and clothing designer Giorgio Armani to Tex-Mex restaurateur Ninfa Laurenzo and spiritual counselor Dorothy Winn, each of these individuals uncovered what they loved to do, what they were good at doing, and ultimately tied it to something greater than themselves. The relevance to our generation is that they did this later in life, when many may have given up on creating the life of their dreams.

Let's face it: everyone on this planet is aging. The universal law is that we are in a constant, never-ending state of entropy. However, the comforting lesson is that our human spirit, our life force, does not age. Despite the ongoing phenomenon of our bodies' aging, our spirits continue to grow, expand, and evolve. There is such power in knowing and embracing this fact. As long as we have *breath*, we have the ability to contribute and to make an impact on the world.

How reassuring to know that even when our lives have been saddled with setback after setback, and we are nearing the last two or three decades of our time here on earth, our spirits can remain resilient. Our spirits have benefited from the experiences of life up until now, and we can now capitalize on the wisdom won through life's many scuffles. With this knowledge, we have the opportunity to create thriving second and third acts in our lives. For the many individuals who may be reading this book and are not where they want to be in life—or perhaps not even who they want to be in life—it is not too late.

Alignment Lessons: Make It Real

- What are you waiting for?

- What is holding you back from taking the seat where you can contribute in a way that makes your heart sing?

- What first step can you take to move in the direction to find your dream seat?

- What mentors or role models can you engage to hold you accountable to execution of that dream?

* * *

My intention in writing this book is to give hope, encouragement, and reassurance to anyone who finds him- or herself at a crossroad in life or in an unwelcome place they never anticipated. "What *am* I going to do *now?*" is the question that trumps any other thoughts. The fifteen remarkable people highlighted in this book experienced tremendous success, by differing definitions, late in life. In many cases, their legacies were created in the last ten years of their time on the planet, when they were most definitely living their last act. The lessons we can derive from their choices, values, and tenacity can inspire us to create our best life.

Each of us has the responsibility to go deep within ourselves and align our soul's intention of how we want to contribute to the world with our gifts and talents. When we tap into this, we live our life with powerful purpose and purposeful power. Each one of us has a destiny to fulfill and a seat to take. It is never too late as long as we have breath.

Everything will be all right in the end. If it's
not all right, it is not yet the end.
—**Patel**, Hotel Manager,
The Best Exotic Marigold Hotel

Sources

Author's Note

Snyder, Michael. "In 2011 The Baby Boomers Start To Turn 65: 16 Statistics About the Coming Retirement Crisis That Will Drop Your Jaw." *The American Dream* (blog). December 30, 2010. http:// endoftheamericandream.com/archives/in-2011-the-baby-boomers -start-to-turn-65-16-statistics-about-the-coming-retirement-crisis-that -will-drop-your-jaw.

Brandon, Emily. "The Baby Boomer Retirement Crunch Begins." *MONEY*. May 13, 2013. http://money.usnews.com/money/retirement /articles/2013/05/13/the-baby-boomer-retirement-crunch-begins.

Perman, Stacy. "Seniors as Entrepreneurs: Their Time Has Come." *Bloomberg Businessweek*. June 8, 2009. http://www.businessweek .com/smallbiz/content/jun2009/sb2009068_927403.htm.

Kinder, George D. "Why you should create a plan for your life." *Wall Street Journal*. October 6, 2007. http://online.wsj.com/ad/fin_plan8.html.

"Resources: 50+ Facts and Fiction." Immersion Active, http://www .immersionactive.com/resources/50-plus-facts-and-fiction/.

Weigelt, David, Jonathan Boehman, and David Wolfe. *Dot Boom: Marketing to Baby Boomers through Meaningful Online Engagement*. Great Falls, VA: LINX Corp, 2009.

Stevenson, Sarah. "Better with Age: 11 Late in Life Success Stories." *A Place for Mom*. October 3, 2013. http://www.aplaceformom.com /blog/2013-10-4-late-in-life-success-stories/.

Penelope. "Posts tagged 'Late life success'." *Don't Hang Up* (blog). http://www.donthangupbook.com/tag/late-life-success/.

Laura Ingalls Wilder: Published Destiny

Wadsworth, Ginger. *Laura Ingalls Wilder—Storyteller of the Prairie*. Minneapolis, MN: Lerner Publications Company, 1997.

Anderson, William T, ed., *Laura Ingalls Wilder and Rose Wilder Lane: a Little House Sampler*. Lincoln, NE: University of Nebraska Press, 1988.

Anderson, William. *Laura Ingalls Wilder—A Biography*. New York: Harper Collins Publishers, 1992.

"Laura Ingalls Wilder." Biography.com. http://www.biography.com /people/laura-ingalls-wilder-9531246.

Anna Mary Robertson: Grandma Moses

Kallir, Jane. "Grandma Moses: The Artist Behind the Myth." *The Clarion* (Fall 1982): 52-55. http://issuu.com/american_folk_art _museum/docs/clarion_fall1982.

Kallir, Otto. *Grandma Moses*. Outlet. November 1986.

Kallir, Otto, ed., *Grandma Moses: My Life's History*. New York: Harper & Brothers, 1952.

Venezia, Mike. *Getting to Know the World's Greatest Artists* (series). Chicago: Children's Press, March 2004.

The Phillips Collection, Washington, D.C.; http://www.phillipscollection .org.

"Grandma Moses." Biography.com. http://www.biography.com/people /grandma-moses-9416251.

Harland Sanders: Kentucky's Unlikely Colonel

Sanders, Harland. *Life As I Have Known It Has Been Finger Lickin' Good*. Lake Mary, FL: Creation House, 1974.

The Colonel Harland Sanders website; http://colonelsanders.com/bio.asp.

The Kentucky Fried Chicken website; http://www.kfc.com/.

"Harland David Sanders." Biography.com. http://www.biography.com
/people/colonel-harland-sanders-12353545.

Barbara Miller: West Texas Live Wire

Rasmussen, Willie. "It's Never Too Late to Start: The Inspiring Story of
Barbara Miller." *Power Homebiz Guide*. May 8, 2000. http://www
.powerhomebiz.com/SBP/texas.htm.

"Civic leader Barbara Miller Dies." *Amarillo Globe-News*. September 6,
2005.

Albright, Max. "Barbara Miller honored for small business award."
Amarillo Globe-News. April 14, 2000.

The Gage Van Horn & Associates website; http://gagevanhorn.com/.

Ray Kroc: Overnight Success

Coleman, Jerry and Steven Garvey. "Ray Kroc: Fast Food Millionaire,"
Biography episode 869, directed by Greg Weinstein. A&E Television
Networks, 1997.

Kroc, Ray and Robert Anderson. *Grinding It Out: The Making of
McDonald's*. New York: St. Martin's Press, 1992.

Hall, M.C. *Ray Kroc (Lives and Times)*. Heinemann, October 1, 2003.

The McDonald's website; www.mcdonalds.com.

"Ray Kroc: Burger Baron." Entrepreneur.com. October 9, 2008. http://
www.entrepreneur.com/article/197544.

Daszkowski, Don. "The Ray Kroc Story—McDonald's Facts and
History." About.com. http://franchises.about.com/od
/mostpopularfranchises/a/ray-kroc-story.htm.

"Ray Kroc Obituary." NYTimes.com. January 15, 1984. http://www
.nytimes.com/learning/general/onthisday/bday/1005.html.

Bill Wilson: From Addiction to Admirable Legacy

Cheever, Susan. *My Name Is Bill: Bill Wilson—His Life and the Creation of Alcoholics Anonymous*. New York: Washington Square Press, 2005.

Woods, James and James Garner. *My Name is Bill W*. Directed by Daniel Petrie. Warner Home Video, 2006.

Hartigan, Francis. *Bill W.: A Biography of Alcoholics Anonymous Cofounder Bill Wilson*. New York: St. Martins Griffin, 2001.

The Alcoholics Anonymous website; www.aa.org/.

Jacqueline Qualls: Writing a New Legacy

Jung, Carl Gustav. *Memories, Dreams, Reflections*. New York: Vintage Books, 1989.

Dorothy Winn: Providential Purpose

Dorothy Winn and Ann Parsley Harper took place in Waxahachie, Texas, on September 27, 2013. Follow-up fact checking by Ann Parsley Harper on 10/23/13, 11/14/13, and 1/15/14.

Li Cunxin: Dancing an Unexpected Life

Kinetz, Erika. "The Dancer Who Defected Twice." *The New York Times*. September 26, 2004.

Warren, Michael. "Li Cunxin: 'Last Dancer' Turned Grateful Defector." *The Washington Times*. April 13, 2011.

Rose, James. "Li Cunxin Continues Journey of Transformation." *The Houston Chronicle*. April 12, 2013.

Cunxin, Li. "Mao's Last Dancer." *Huffington Post Arts & Culture*. August 27, 2010. http://www.huffingtonpost.com/li-cunxin /post_758_b_697605.html.

Cao, Chi and Bruce Greenwood. *Mao's Last Dancer*. Directed by Bruce Beresford, 2009. DVD.

The Li Cunxin website; http://www.licunxin.com.

"Li Cunxin—Mao's Last Dancer." YouTube.com. September 28, 2009. https://www.youtube.com/watch?v=UbIFdwViKcU.

Diana Nyad: Roaring with Resilience

Weil, Elizabeth. "Marathon Swimmer Diana Nyad Takes on the Demons of the Sea." *The New York Times*. December 1, 2011.

"The Other Shore: the Diana Nyad Story." Showtime Documentary. Directed by Timothy Wheeler, 2013.

The Savvy Traveler website; http://savvytraveler.publicradio.org.

Diana Nyad (all posts). *The Huffington Post*. www.huffingtonpost.com /diana-nyad.

The Diana Nyad website; www.diananyad.com.

Nyad, Diana. "Never, ever give up." *TED Talks*. December, 2013. http:// www.ted.com/talks/diana_nyad_never_ever_give_up.

Frank McCourt: To and From the Ashes

McCourt, Frank. *Angela's Ashes*. New York: Scribner, 1999.

McCourt, Frank. *'Tis: A Memoir*. New York: Simon and Schuster, 2000.

Watson, Emily, Robert Carlyle, and Joe Breen. *Angela's Ashes*. Directed by Alan Parker. David Brown Productions, 1999. DVD.

"Francis McCourt." Biography.com. http://www.biography.com/people /frank-mccourt-9391286.

The PBS website; www.pbs.org/onlyateacher.

Grimes, William. "Frank McCourt is Dead at 78." *The New York Times*. July 29, 2009.

Ninfa Laurenzo: Autumn Season Success

Sharpe, Patricia. "We Remember Ninfa Laurenzo." *Texas Monthly*. August, 2001.

Morago, Greg. "Remembering Ninfa." *The Houston Chronicle*. May 12, 2014.

Kaplan, David. "Two Mama Ninfa Legacies, Side by Side." *The Houston Chronicle*. October 30, 2012.

The El Tiempo Cantina website; www.eltiempocantina.com.

Kathryn Joosten: Carpool to Credits

Furlong, Maggie. "Kathryn Joosten Dead: 'Desperate Housewives' Star Dies at 72." *The Huffington Post*. June 2, 2012.

"Kathryn Joosten Dies at 72." *The New York Times*. June 3, 2012.

Nelson, Valerie J. "'Desperate Housewives' actress who played Mrs. McCluskey Dies." *Los Angeles Times*. June 3, 2012.

McGinnis, Sara. "Kathryn Joosten Dies At Age 72." *SheKnows*. June 2, 2012. http://www.sheknows.com/entertainment/articles/961993 /kathryn-joosten-mrs-mccluskey-on-desperate-housewives-dies-from -cancer.

"Kathryn Joosten." *TV Guide*. http://www.tvguide.com/celebrities /kathryn-joosten/249360.

"'Desperate Housewives' Kathryn Joosten's Last Interview." YouTube.com. June 2, 2012. https://www.youtube.com/watch?v=WYO7qi2WhdM.

Giorgio Armani: The Calm Couturier

Kroll, Betsy. "He Creates Everything." *TIME Magazine*. September 15, 2009.

Cocks, Jay. "Giorgio Armani: Suiting up for East Street." *TIME Magazine*. April 5, 1982.

Galloni, Alessandra, and Christina Passariello. "Armani's One Man Brand." *Wall Street Journal*. April 20, 2006.

"Giorgio Armani (profile)." *Forbes*. June 25, 2014. http://www.forbes.com /profile/giorgio-armani/.

"Giorgio Armani." Biography.com. http://www.biography.com/people /giorgio-armani-9188652.

"Biography: Giorgio Armani." *Lifetime TV*. http://www.lifetimetv.co.uk /biography/biography-giorgio-armani.

"Giorgio Armani Biography." *The Famous People*. http://www .thefamouspeople.com/profiles/giorgio-armani-3346.php.

Wally Blume: The Ice Cream Man

"Late Bloomers," Entrepreneur.com, May 27, 2010.

Perman, Stacy. " Seniors as Entrepreneurs, Their Time Has Come." *Bloomberg Businessweek*. June 8, 2009.

Carlozo, Lou. "How to Make a Fortune After 50." Reuters.com. December 23, 2011.

Terhune, Linda Thomas. "Making Tracks." *Krannert Magazine*. Purdue Krannert School of Management. Fall, 2009.

www.moosetracks.com

Deneen, Sally. "Too Late to Start a Business?" *Success Magazine*. July 27, 2010.

"How I Made My Millions," www.cnbc.com.

"The Blumes: The Open Doors of the Occult." www.cbn.com/700club.

"They Struck it Rich After 50," ABC News. May 20, 2010.

Afterword:

Campell, Joseph and Bill Moyer, *The Power of Myth*, Anchor, 1991.

The Hero's Journey: Joseph Campbell on his Life and Work. New World Library, Third Edition, March 2014.

Frankl, Victor. *Man's Search for Meaning*. Beacon Press, June 2006.

Suggested Reading for Re-Alignment

Adams, Marilee. *Change your Questions Change your Life.* San Francisco, CA: Berrett-Koehler Publishers, 2004.

Bodian, Stephan. *Wake Up Now.* New York: McGraw Hill, 2008.

Campbell, Joseph. *The Hero's Journey.* Novato, CA: New World Library, 2003.

Chodron, Pema. *Start Where You Are.* Boston: Shambhala, 1994.

Cloud, Henry. *Necessary Endings.* New York: Harper Collins Publishers, 2010.

Frankl, Victor. *Man's Search for Meaning.* Boston: Beacon, 2000.

Gibbons, Leeza. *Take 2.* Carlsbad, CA: Hay House, Inc. 2013.

Hanh, Thich Nhat. *The Miracle of Mindfulness.* Boston: Beacon, 1975.

Holden, Daniel. *Lost Between Lives.* West Harford, CT: WingFire, 2004.

Hopson, Barrie, and Katie Ledger. *And What Do You Do?,* London: A&C Black Publishers, 2009.

Houline, Tim, and Tom Maxwell. *The New World of Work*. Irving, TX: Inspire on Purpose, 2013.

Jung, Carl. *The Undiscovered Self*. New York: First Signet, 2006.

Kaufman, Kristin. *Is This Seat Taken?*. Dallas, TX: Brown Books Publishing, 2011.

Kubler-Ross, Elisabeth. *Life Lessons*. New York: Touchstone, 2000.

Lao Tzu and Stephen Mitchell. *Tao Te Ching*. New York: Harper Perennial Classics, 2006.

McGraw, Phil. *Life Code*. New York: Bird Street Books, 2012.

Reivich, Karen, and Andrew Shatt. *The Resilience Factor*. New York: Broadway Books, 2002.

Roche-Terry, Dona, and Dale Roche-Lebrec. *What's Next?* New York: Palgrave Macmillan, 2011.

The Ryrie Study Bible, King James Version. Chicago: Moody, 1978.

Singer, Michael A. *The Untethered Soul*. Oakland, CA: New Harbinger Publications, 2007.

Strozzi Heckler, Richard. *Holding the Center*. Berkeley, CA: North Atlantic Books, 1997.

Suzuki, Shunrya. *Zen Mind, Beginner's Mind*. Boston, MA: Shambhala Press, 2011.

Teasdale, Wayne, and Ken Wilbur. *A Monk in the World*. Novato, CA: New World Library, 2002.

Tolle, Eckhart. *The Power of Now*. Novato, CA: New World Library, 1999.

Warren, Rick. *The Purpose Driven Life*. Grand Rapids, MI: Zondervan, 2002.

Wilbur, Ken. *The Essential Ken Wilbur*. Boston: Shambhala, 2008.

About the Author

Kristin Kaufman is the founder of Alignment, Inc.,® a unique consultancy committed to increasing alignment within individuals, teams, boards, and organizations in order to release their potential into the marketplace and the world, and to creating sustainable success individually and collectively. Serving as a catalyst for development and tapping into potential brings her tremendous fulfillment. She's brought her passion and expertise to thousands of people since establishing Alignment, Inc.®

In addition to her consultancy, Kaufman models alignment by integrating a thriving direct sales business into her life. An avid proponent of the Rodan+Fields business model and product offering, this additional endeavor enables her to offer entrepreneurship as a vehicle for individual alignment, personal growth, and financial independence.

Kaufman has held senior executive positions at Hewlett-Packard, Vignette Corporation, and United Healthgroup. She also offered her skills and talents to the New York City Leadership Academy effort, which was the centerpiece of Mayor Michael Bloomberg and Chancellor Joel Klein's school reform platform.

She has been awarded the distinction of Professional Certified Coach from the International Coaching Federation and achieved the designation of Certified Leadership Coach from Georgetown University's Institute for Transformational Leadership.

Kaufman is a prolific writer. Her first book in the "Is This Seat Taken?" series centered on her global experiences seeding her own journey to alignment. It was released to national acclaim. She resides in Dallas with her rescued white schnauzer and constant companion, LuLu.

Kristin Kaufman may be found at:

www.kristinkaufman.com

www.alignmentinc.com

www.kristinkaufman.myrandf.com

www.linkedin.com/in/kristinskaufman

www.twitter.com/kristinkaufman

www.pinterest.com/kristinkaufman/

www.facebook.com/kristin.kaufman